CHILDREN'S ENCYCLOPEDIA

THE WORLD OF KNOWLEDGE

HUMAN BODY

Manasvi Vohra

V&S PUBLISHERS

Published by:

V&S PUBLISHERS

F-2/16, Ansari road, Daryaganj, New Delhi-110002
☎ 23240026, 23240027 • *Fax:* 011-23240028
Email: info@vspublishers.com • *Website:* www.vspublishers.com

Regional Office : Hyderabad
5-1-707/1, Brij Bhawan (Beside Central Bank of India Lane)
Bank Street, Koti, Hyderabad - 500 095
☎ 040-24737290
E-mail: vspublishershyd@gmail.com

Branch Office : Mumbai
Jaywant Industrial Estate, 1st Floor–108, Tardeo Road
Opposite Sobo Central Mall, Mumbai – 400 034
☎ 022-23510736
E-mail: vspublishersmum@gmail.com

Follow us on: 🇹 f in

DISCLAIMER

While every attempt has been made to provide accurate and timely information in this book, neither the author nor the publisher assumes any responsibility for errors, unintended omissions or commissions detected therein. The author and publisher makes no representation or warranty with respect to the comprehensiveness or completeness of the contents provided.

All matters included have been simplified under professional guidance for general information only, without any warranty for applicability on an individual. Any mention of an organization or a website in the book, by way of citation or as a source of additional information, doesn't imply the endorsement of the content either by the author or the publisher. It is possible that websites cited may have changed or removed between the time of editing and publishing the book.

Results from using the expert opinion in this book will be totally dependent on individual circumstances and factors beyond the control of the author and the publisher.

It makes sense to elicit advice from well informed sources before implementing the ideas given in the book. The reader assumes full responsibility for the consequences arising out from reading this book.

For proper guidance, it is advisable to read the book under the watchful eyes of parents/guardian. The buyer of this book assumes all responsibility for the use of given materials and information.

The copyright of the entire content of this book rests with the author/publisher. Any infringement/transmission of the cover design, text or illustrations, in any form, by any means, by any entity will invite legal action and be responsible for consequences thereon.

PUBLISHER'S NOTE

V&S Publishers is glad to announce the launch of a unique, set of 12 books under the head, *Children's Encyclopedia – The World of Knowledge.* The set of 12 books namely – *Physices, Chemistry, Space Science, General Sceince, Life Science, Human Body, Electronics & Communications, Scientists, Inventions & Discoveries, Transportation, The Earth, and GK (General Knowledge)* has been especially developed keeping in mind the students and children of all age groups, particularly from 6 to 14 years of age. Our main aim is to arouse the interest and solve the queries of the school children regarding the various and diverse topics of Science and help them master the subject thoroughly.

In the book, *Human Body,* the author focusses mainly on the detailed study of the *Human Body, The Internal Organs, The External Organs, Our Body Systems* and so on...

Each chapter is followed by a section called **Quick Facts** that contains a set of interesting and fascinating facts about the topics already discussed in the chapter. There are also **Exercises** compiled at the end of the book followed by a **Glossary** of difficult words and scientific terms to make the book complete and comprehensive.

Quick Facts

> * A poison arrow frog has so much poison in it that it can harm about 2200 people in one squirt.

Though our aim is to be flawless, but errors might have crept in inadvertently. So we request our esteemed readers to read the book thoroughly and offer valuable suggestions wherever necessary to improve and enhance the quality of the book. Hope it interests you all and serves its purpose well.

CONTENTS

HUMAN BODY

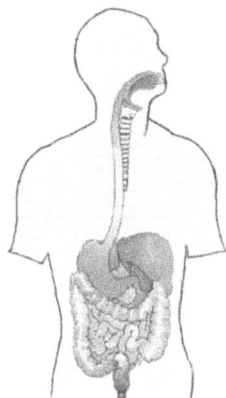

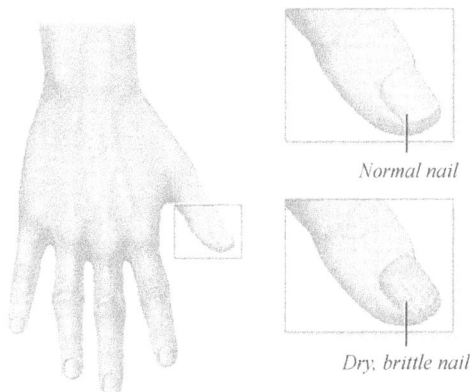

Normal nail

Dry, brittle nail

THE HUMAN BODY

The human body is the entire structure of a human organism, and consists of a head, neck, torso, two arms and two legs. By the time, the human being (man or woman) reaches adulthood, the body consists of close to *100 trillion cells*, the basic unit of life. These cells are organised biologically to eventually form the whole body.

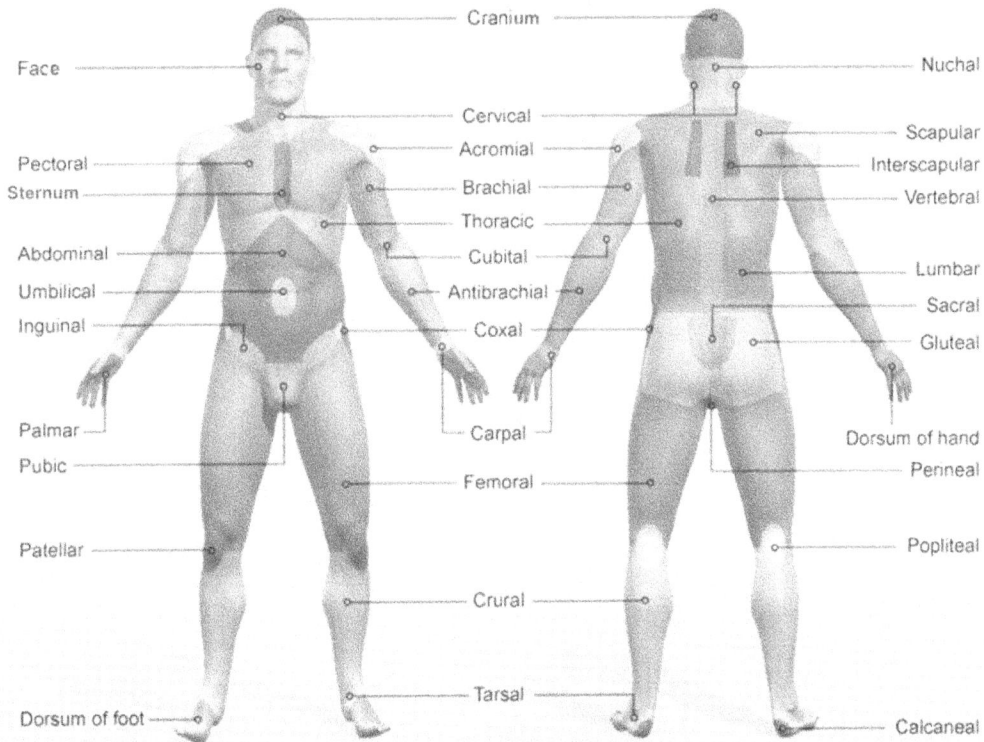

Cranium

Face

Nuchal

Cervical

Scapular

Acromial

Interscapular

Pectoral

Brachial

Vertebral

Sternum

Thoracic

Abdominal

Cubital

Lumbar

Umbilical

Antibrachial

Sacral

Inguinal

Coxal

Gluteal

Palmar

Carpal

Dorsum of hand

Pubic

Penneal

Femoral

Patellar

Popliteal

Crural

Tarsal

Dorsum of foot

Calcaneal

Parts of the Body

Size, Type and Proportion

The average height of an adult male human is about 1.7–1.8 m (5'7" to 5'11") tall and the adult female about 1.6–1.7 m (5'2" to 5'7") tall. This size is firstly determined by genes and secondly, by diet. Body type and body composition are influenced by post-natal factors, such as diet and exercise.

Organ Systems

The organ systems of the body include the musculoskeletal system, cardiovascular system, digestive system, endocrine system, integumentary system, urinary system, lymphatic system, immune system,

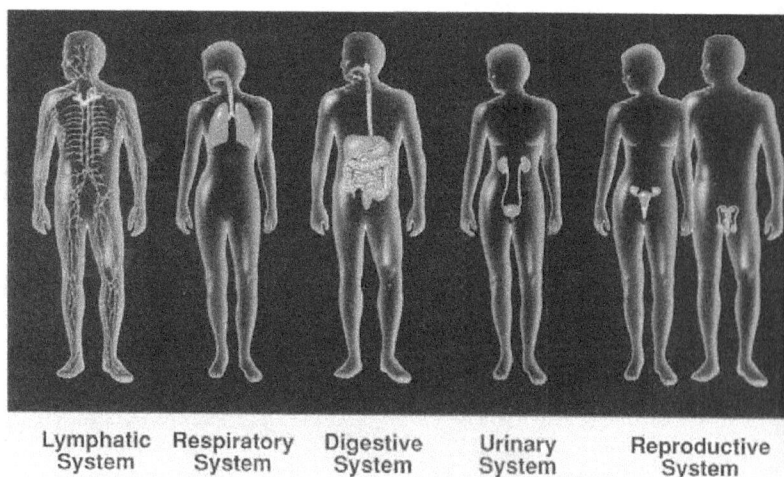

Lymphatic System   Respiratory System   Digestive System   Urinary System   Reproductive System

respiratory system, nervous system and the reproductive system.

Constituents of the Human Body

In a normal man weighing 60 kg

Constituents	Weight	Percent of atoms
Oxygen	38.8 kg	25.5 %
Carbon	10.9 kg	9.5 %
Hydrogen	6.0 kg	63 %
Nitrogen	1.9 kg	1.4 %
Calcium	1.2 kg	0.2%
Phosphorus	0.6 kg	0.2 %
Potassium	0.2 kg	0.07 %

Part - I

THE INTERNAL ORGANS

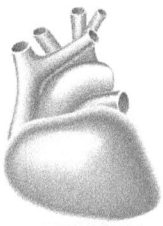

Heart

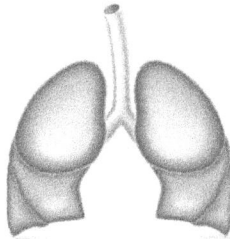

Lungs

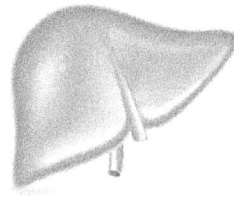

Liver

Stomach

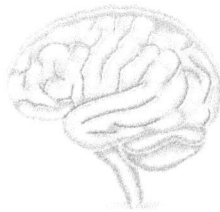

Brain

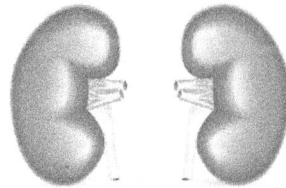

Kidneys

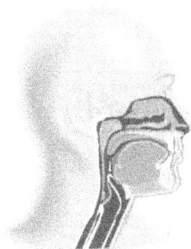

Trachea and Oesophagus

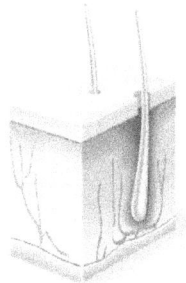

Skin

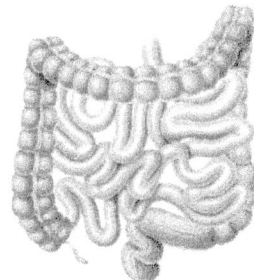

Small Intestine

Chapter - 1

THE CELLS

The human body is formed by millions of tiny units called *cells*. Each of these tiny units has a specific shape, size and function to perform. There are more than 200 types of cells known till today. These cells function together and perform all the actions of the human body. The millions of cells in the body practise division of labour and hence, various groups of cells perform the different functions of the human body. Cells that perform a particular function together are called tissues.

A thin membrane, called as the cell membrane, surrounds each individual cell. It performs the job of regulating things like

Endoplasmic Redticulum

Nucleus

Nucleolus

Golgi Apparatus

Microtubules

Miltochandria

Lysosomes

Microfilaments

Secretory Granules

The Human Cell

nutrients and other substances in and out of the cell. Cells multiply by dividing continually into two identical offsprings. It is through this division process that the body is able to grow and replace the damaged or worn out cells.

The broad categories of the kinds of cells in the human body are:

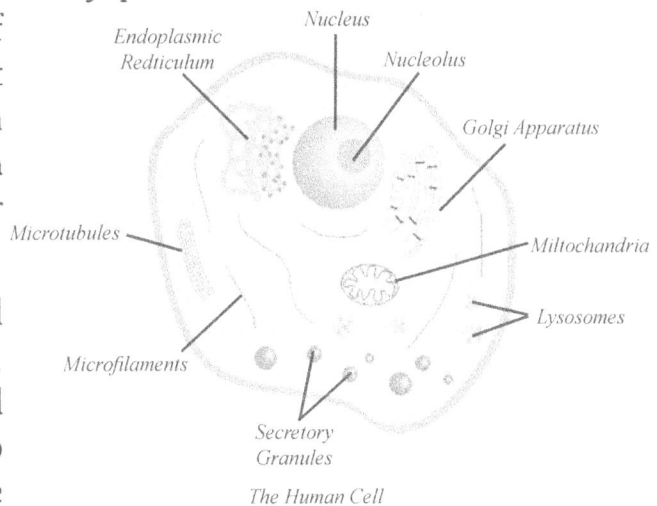

1. Nerve Cells

These are one of the most important kinds of cells in the body. These are called **Neurons**, and are found in the *brain*, *spinal cord* and the *nerves*. They are responsible for carrying high-speed electrical signals, called nerve impulses. It is due to these impulses that our body processes coordinate and we are able to think, feel and move. There are two types of nerves functioning in the human body. The *Sensory Nerves* which contain the Sensory Nerve Cells bringing signals and information to the brain and the **Motor Nerves** containing the Motor Nerve Cells carrying orders and messages from the brain to the various organs and parts of the body.

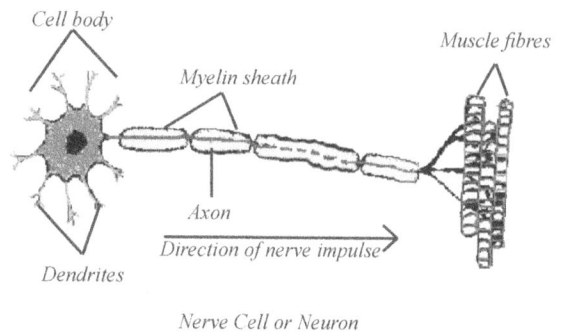

Nerve Cell or Neuron

2. White Blood Cells (WBCs)

These cells are called the soldiers of the human body. Circulating in the *blood* and a clear fluid called *lymph*, these cells are responsible for fighting the diseases that attack the human body. These cells consist of *macrophages* and *neutrophils*, which perform the job of eating bacteria and other germs. Also, these cells contain **lymphocytes**, which release germ-disabling antibodies.

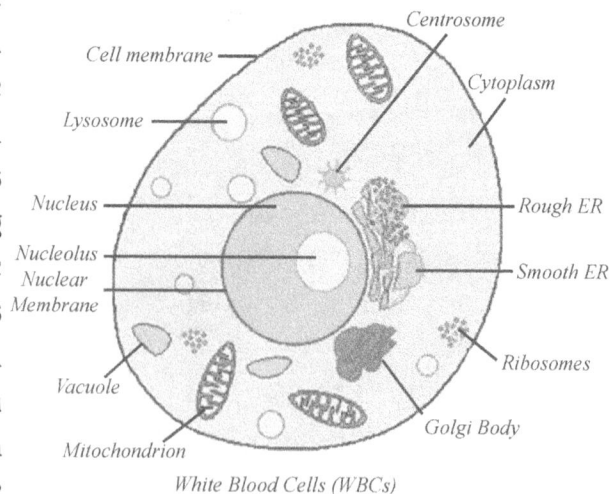

White Blood Cells (WBCs)

3. Red Blood Cells (RBCs)

The Red blood cells, or Erythrocytes, are the most common type of blood cells, and the vertebrate organism's principal means of delivering oxygen (O_2) to the body tissues through the blood flow or the circulatory system.

Red Blood Cells (RBCs)

They take up oxygen in the lungs or gills and release it while squeezing through the body's capillaries. These cells' cytoplasm is rich in **haemoglobin**, an iron-containing biomolecule that can bind oxygen and is responsible for the blood's red colour.

In humans, mature red blood cells are oval and flexible biconcave disks. They lack a cell nucleus and most organelles to accommodate maximum space for haemoglobin. About 2.4 million new **erythrocytes** are produced per second. The cells develop in the bone marrow and circulate for about 100–120 days in the body before their components are recycled by macrophages. Each circulation takes about 20 seconds. Approximately, a quarter of the cells in the human body are **Red Blood Cells** or **RBCs**.

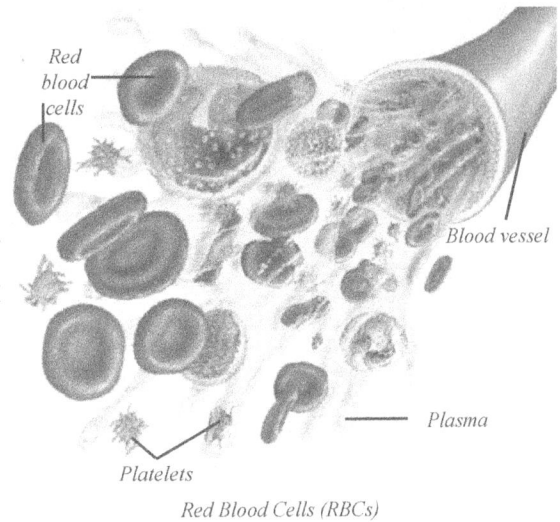

4. Epithelial Cells

These cells cover the human body as they form the outer layer of the skin. They also line the hollow organs, such as the stomach, lungs and the bladder. These are tightly packed together and are responsible for stopping harmful chemicals and germs from reaching the body tissues.

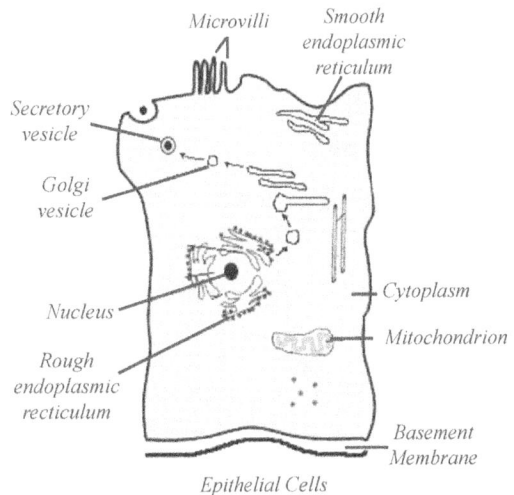

Epithelial Cells

5. Bone Cells or Osteocytes

These are the bone cells that help keep the bones in a good condition. They primarily lay down as bones, but later get stranded in the body spaces. They stay connected through thread like veins and arteries, and blood supplies from the surrounding blood vessels.

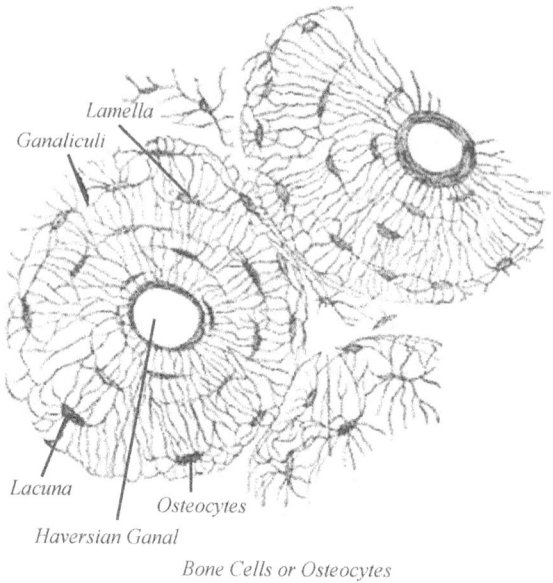

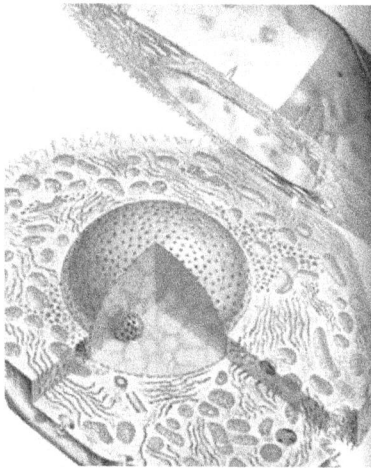

Lamella
Ganaliculi
Lacuna
Osteocytes
Haversian Ganal

Bone Cells or Osteocytes

Liver cells or Hepatocytes

6. Liver Cells or Hepatocytes

These cells are responsible for enabling the liver to perform functions, such as controlled blood composition and maintain stability in the body. Also called as **Hepatocytes**, they process and stored food and remove the poisonous waste from the liver.

7. Fat Cells

These cells group together to form the **Adipose tissue** and store fat. They store energy and also cushion the various organs, such as the kidneys. They also insulate the body from under the skin.

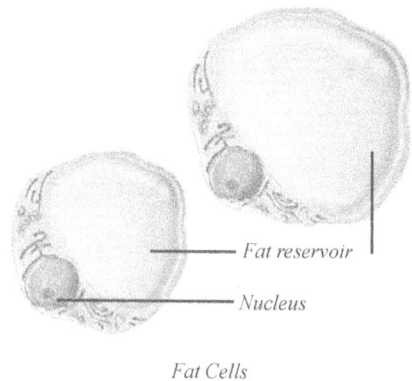

Fat reservoir
Nucleus

Fat Cells

- One can grow heart cells in a petri dish.

- The human body is made up of 100 trillion cells. Each cell has at least one nucleus, which houses the chromosomes.

- There is 1.8 m of DNA in each of our cells packed into a structure only 0.0001 cm across (it would easily fit on the head of a pin).

- If all the DNA in the 100 trillion cells of the human body was put end to end, it would reach to the sun and back over 600 times [100 trillion × 6 ft (1.8 m) divided by 92 million miles (148 800 000 km) = 1200].

- Most human cells contain 46 chromosomes: pairs of chromosomes 1-22, and a pair of sex chromosomes (females have two Xs; males -- an X and a Y). The sperm and eggs contain one of each chromosome.

Chapter - 2

BLOOD

The red liquid flowing all around our body is called the blood. It is probably the most important part of the human body as it is the blood that performs the most vital functions of the body. Circulating in **arteries** and **veins**, the blood carries *food, oxygen* and other *essential substances* around the body. It also carries cells and removes their wastes. Moreover, it is responsible for providing heat to the body and defends it against diseases and infections. In an average human body, around **5 litres** of blood circulates at any given time.

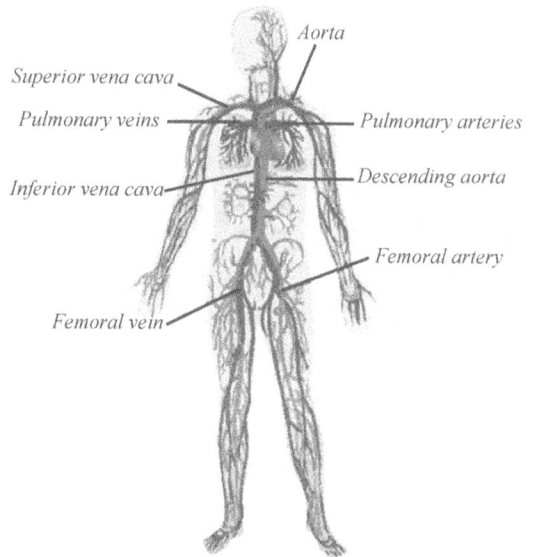

Aorta
Superior vena cava
Pulmonary veins
Pulmonary arteries
Descending aorta
Inferior vena cava
Femoral artery
Femoral vein

Circulatory System of the Human Body

The human blood is made out of a yellow liquid called the **plasma** and it flows in the same. The plasma is formed of 90% water and the rest 10% consists of various dissolved substances like food, salts, hormones, etc. Further, the blood consists of 55% plasma and the rest is constituted of blood cells.

Various blood cells perform different functions. The **Red Blood Cells (RBCs)** carry oxygen from the lungs to the rest of the body. Every second, two million Red Cells are produced in the human body. The **White Blood Cells (WBCs)**, called *neutrophils* and *macrophages* eat germs and protect us against diseases. They release antibodies that fight germs in our body.

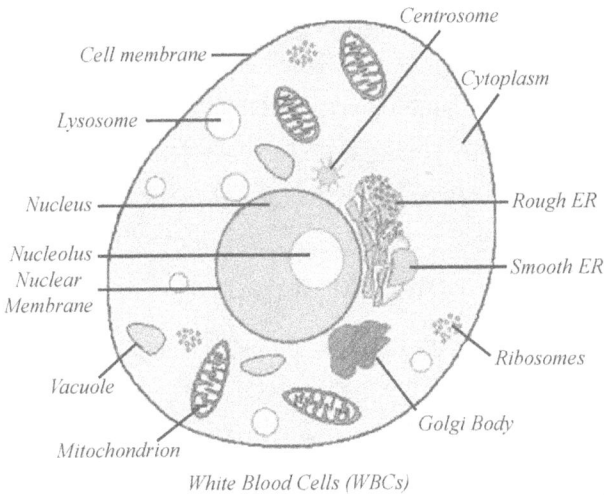

White Blood Cells (WBCs)

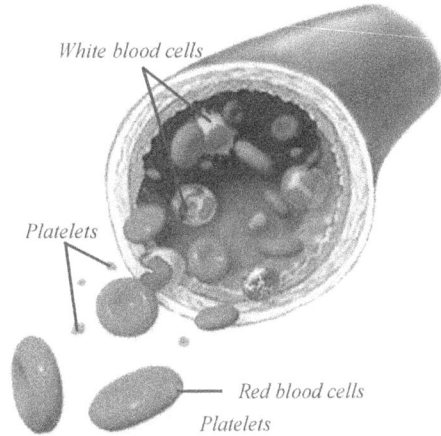

Another element of the blood, called the **platelets** perform the job of clotting the damaged blood vessels. It is interesting to know that each drop of blood consists of about 250 million Red Blood Cells (RBCs), around 375,000 White Blood Cells (WBCs) and 1 million platelets.

The **heart** pumps the blood. The human heart is made up of mainly *cardiac muscles* which do not tire. The **veins** bring deoxygenated blood to the heart which then oxygenates it and pumps out to the body through the **arteries**. On an average, the human heart beats **72 times**

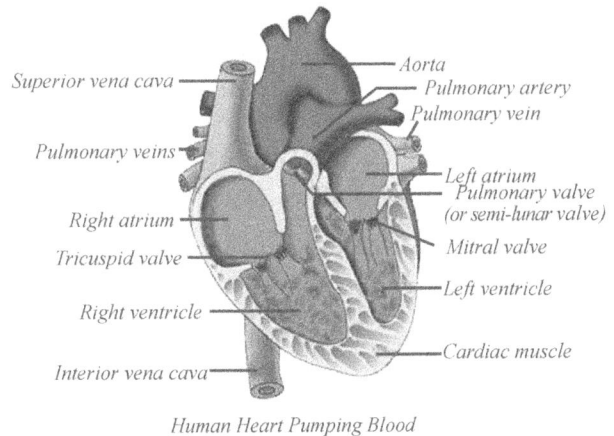

Human Heart Pumping Blood

in a minute. However, this rating may increase to double or even triple due to excessive physical activity as then, the heart pumps blood

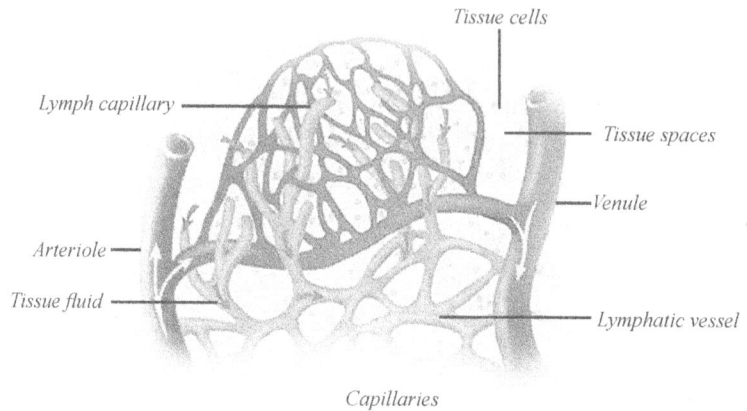

Capillaries

Labels: Tissue cells, Lymph capillary, Tissue spaces, Venule, Arteriole, Lymphatic vessel, Tissue fluid

Artery

Labels: Normal artery, Artery narrowed by atheroselerosis, Plaque, Bllod flow

faster to send more oxygen to our muscles. It is a fact that over a lifetime of 70 years, the heart beat 2.5 billion times without taking a break.

Among the blood vessels, the arteries carry pure blood away from the heart, while the veins bring the impure blood

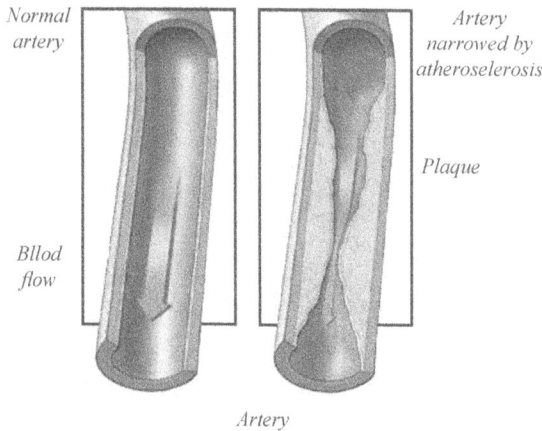

from the different organs back to it. Microscopic **capillaries** link the arteries and veins to provide blood to the cells. The arteries carry bright-red coloured blood as it is oxygenated, whereas the veins carry the deoxygenated blood, which is dull-purple in colour. It

Blood Vessel

Labels: Arteriole, Venule, Capillary, Valve, Inner layer, Middle layer, Outer layer, Artery, Vein

would interest you to know that if stretched out, one adult's blood vessels would encircle the Earth twice and the capillaries would make up about 98 percent of the total length.

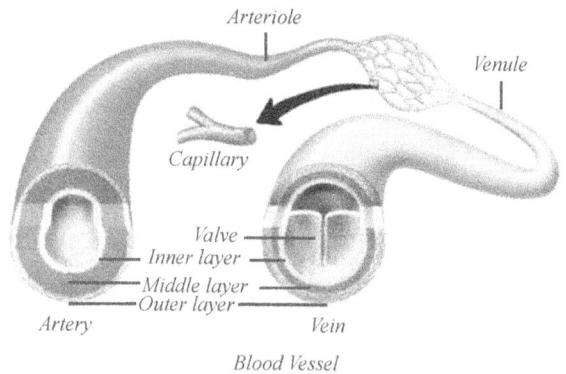

- Blood makes up around 10 percent of our body weight. Our weight divided by 12 tells us how many pints of blood our body has.

- Blood cells float in a yellow liquid called blood plasma. This is made up of 90% water and also contains various nutrients, proteins, glucose and hormones.

- Blood is about twice as thick as water, thanks to all the cells and other bits that float in it.

- Blood makes up about 10 percent of your body weight. Weigh yourself and divide your weight by 12 - that answer is about how many pints of blood your body has. Adults usually have roughly 10 to 15 pints. A newborn baby has about one-half pint or one cup of blood.

- It takes roughly 20 to 60 seconds for the blood to travel away from the heart and back again.

Chapter - 3

THE BRAIN

The brain is one of the most vital organs of the human body. Resting inside the skull, it enables us to *think, sense, learn, move* and *remember*. It also regulates other important processes of the body, such as breathing, etc.

The main part of the human brain, called the **cerebrum** is divided into two hemispheres. While the right hemisphere controls the left side of the body and deals with art, music and creativity, the left side, controls the right side of the body and is responsible for mathematics, language and problem solving. The outer layer of the cerebrum, known as the **cortex**, performs all its tasks. The cortex has different roles at distinct areas of the brain. So,

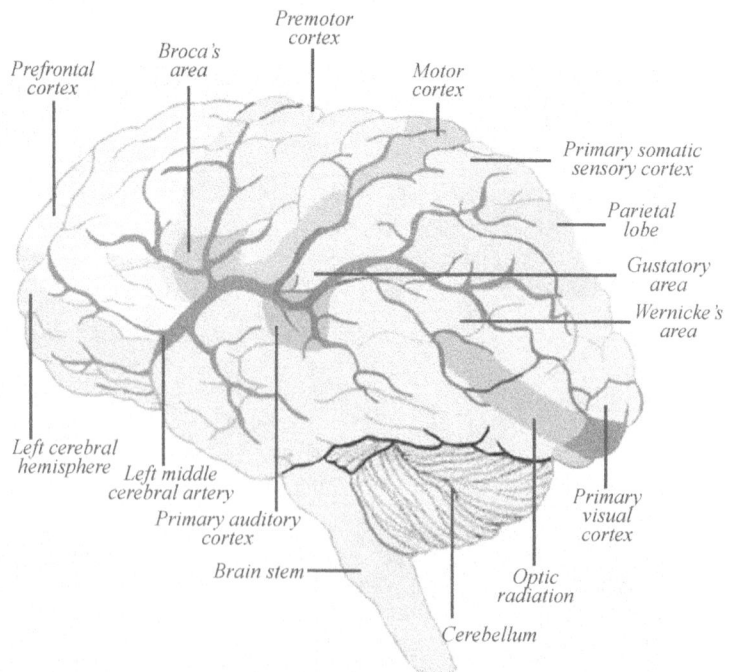

The Human Brain

the motor areas trigger movements, the association areas interpret functions, the sensory areas deal with senses and so on.

Some of the parts of the Brain and their functions are as follows:-

1. **Prefrontal Cortex:** This is the most complex part of the cerebrum and is responsible for what we are. It allows us to reason, plan, create and learn about thoughts and ideas and gives us the sense of having a *conscience*. Hence, it is responsible for our personality and intellect.

2. **Broca's area:** This is usually placed in the left hemisphere, and is responsible for *planning* what we are about to say and accordingly sends out instructions to the muscles in the throat, tongue and lips to produce speech. It was named after *Dr. Paul Broca*, who discovered it.

3. **Premotor Cortex:** This part of the brain controls all the *movement skills*, for example, playing tennis or swimming, etc. At the time of physical movement, it instructs the specific muscles to contract, etc. either through the primary motor cortex or directly.

4. **Primary Motor Cortex:** Most of the movement of the human body is regulated by the primary motor cortex. It *receives information* from the *cerebellum* and other parts of the brain and instructs the muscles to move and in a particular sequence.

5. **Cerebellum:** This part of the human brain performs the task of enabling *smooth and coordinated movements*. After analysing the incoming information about the body's current position, it interacts with the primary motor cortex to time the muscle contractions precisely.

6. **Primary Visual Cortex:** As light hits the back of the retina in each eye, the light detectors send a signal to the primary visual cortex. It then *interprets* the basic shapes, sizes and colour and passes it on to the visual association cortex.

7. **Visual Association Cortex:** This is the place where *information* of the primary visual cortex is analysed and *compared* to previous experiences. It identifies what and where we are looking, enabling us to actually *see* things.

8. **Primary Sensory Cortex:** There are receptors in our skin which send signals regarding touch, vibration, etc. enabling us to *feel* them. Lips and fingertips have more receptors and hence, they are extra sensitive.

9. **Sensory Association Cortex:** The information about touch or any kind of sensation is passed to the sensory association cortex by the primary sensory cortex. It is then *analysed and interpreted* before being compared to past experiences.

10. **Primary Auditory Cortex:** Sounds detected by the ears are transferred to the primary auditory cortex, where the *loudness, pitch, etc. are identified*. Then the information is passed to the auditory association cortex.

11. **Auditory Association Cortex:** This is where *sounds* are actually *heard*. Using signals from the primary auditory cortex, it joins the pieces together to form complete sounds and *identifies* it as music, speech, etc.

12. **Wernicke's Area:** It is usually found in the left hemisphere of the cerebrum, it *gives meaning to the words that are heard or read*. It is directly linked to the Broca's area, which enables *speech*.

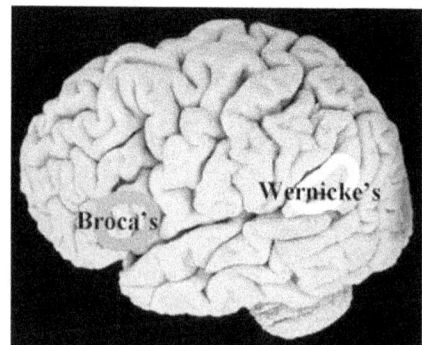

Wernicke's Area of the Cerebrum

Quick Facts

- The human brain is like a powerful computer that stores our memory and controls how we as humans think and react. It has evolved over time and features some incredibly intricate parts that scientists still struggle to understand.

- The brain has no pain receptors and hence, cannot feel any pain.

- The brain can process information as slowly as 0.5 metres/sec or as fast as 120 metres/sec.

- The brain is the centre of the human nervous system, controlling our thoughts, movements, memories and decisions.

- The brain contains billions of nerve cells that send and receive information around the body.

- The human brain is over three times as big as the brain of other mammals that are of similar body size.

Chapter - 4

THE SENSES

The human body constitutes of **five senses** which enable us to be a part of the world around us and observe and notice the changes that occur in it. Our eyes and ears detect *light waves* and *sound waves* respectively. These allow us to see and hear. The tongue and the nose perform the task of detecting dissolved chemicals so that we can *taste, smell* and hence, enjoy flavours. The skin allows us to *feel* the texture and *warmth* of the objects that surround us.

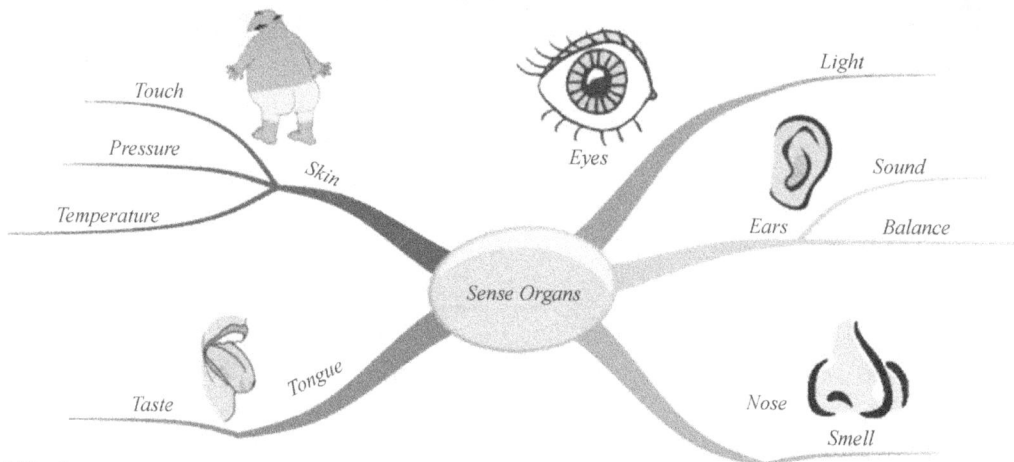

Vision

This is the most important sense as it provides the brain immense amount of knowledge about the body's surroundings. The light that

is reflected or produced by objects that surround us is focussed on a layer of light receptors that exist at the back of our eyes. These receptors send the light signals to the back of the brain, where the images are developed and interpreted. Signals are then sent back to the eye, enabling us to *see* objects around us.

Hearing

The receptors in the ears detect the waves of pressure, or *sound waves* that travel through the air. These waves are created by things around us, like a bell ringing or a mobile phone vibrating. These waves pass into the inner part of the ear which is enclosed in a bone at the side of the skull. This is where the *receptors* convert the *waves into signals* that travel through the brain. The brain then interprets the *loudness, pitch,* etc. and completes the sound for us to hear.

Taste

Our tongue has got numerous projections on its surface, called the *papillae*. These are a home to the taste receptors, called the *taste buds*. When food molecules dissolve in *saliva*, the taste buds detect them. Taste can be distinguished as *sweet, bitter, sour, salty,* etc. Apart from tasting, these receptors also help us to detect any kind of poison that may be present in the food.

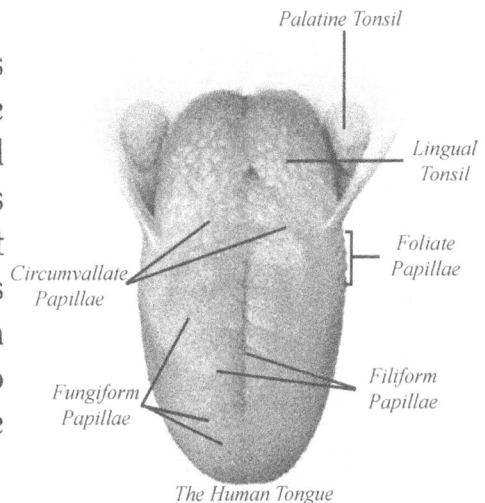

Palatine Tonsil

Lingual Tonsil

Foliate Papillae

Circumvallate Papillae

Filiform Papillae

Fungiform Papillae

The Human Tongue

Touch

Human *skin* is like a sense organ. It has got innumerable receptors all over its surface, enabling us to feel our surroundings. Most of these are *touch receptors* that send signals to the brain and allow us to feel things. Other receptors pick up changes in *temperature*, etc.

Smell

It is a fact that the human nose can detect up to *10,000 different smells*. When we breathe air, the odour molecules dissolved in mucus act as receptors and pick up the smell. Together, taste and smell enable us to enjoy flavours. This is the reason why food seems flavourless when we have a blocked nose.

Quick Facts

- **After eating, our hearing power decreases.**

- **About one-third of the human race has 20-20 vision. Glasses and contact wearers are hardly alone in a world where two thirds of the population have less than perfect vision. The amount of people with perfect vision decreases further as they age.**

- **If our saliva cannot dissolve something, you cannot taste it. In order for foods, or anything else, to have a taste, chemicals from the substance must be dissolved by saliva. If you don't believe it, try drying off your tongue before tasting something.**

- **Your nose can remember about 50,000 different scents.**

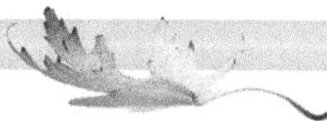

PART - II

OUR BODY SYSTEMS

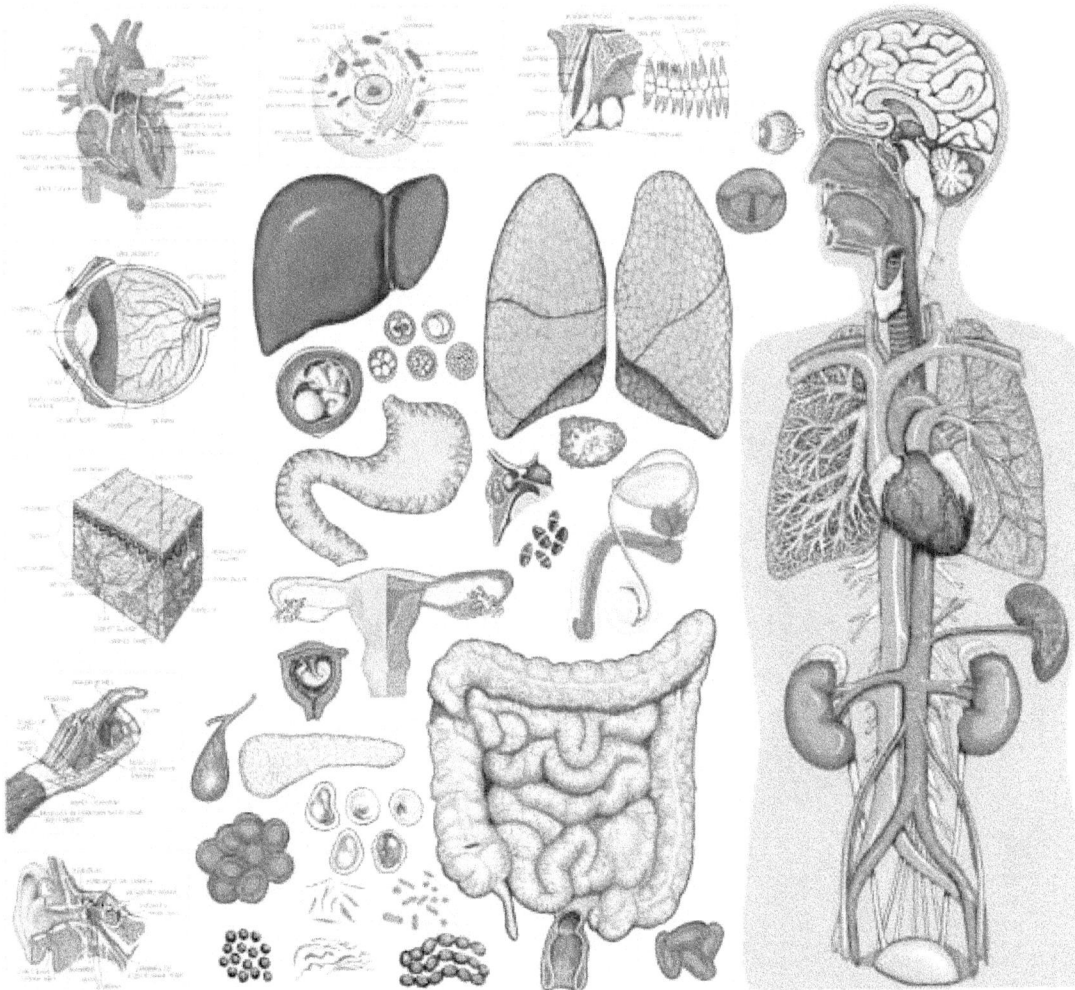

Chapter - 1

THE RESPIRATORY SYSTEM

The respiratory system of the body is responsible for one of the major functions of the body. It is through this process that the trillion of cells in our body receive oxygen that they need to survive. In a broad sense, oxygenated air is breathed into the body by the respiratory system. Air with **oxygen** reaches the blood through the lungs and is further carried to the blood cells, while the waste **carbon dioxide** is carried by the blood to the lungs and breathed out.

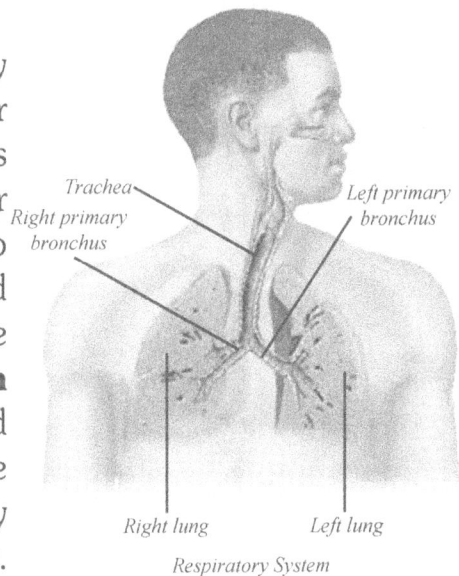

Trachea
Right primary bronchus
Left primary bronchus
Right lung
Left lung

Respiratory System

The prime responsibility of the respiratory system is to *supply blood with oxygen*. The blood then delivers this oxygen to the various parts of the body. The respiratory system does this through the process of **breathing**. When we breathe, we *inhale oxygen* and *exhale carbon dioxide* and it is through this exchange of gases that the respiratory system is able to get oxygen into the blood.

The process of respiration involves the use of the *mouth*, *nose*, *trachea*, *lungs*, and the *diaphragm*. Oxygen enters the human body through the mouth and the nose. It then passes through the larynx, the area where speech sounds are produced and the trachea which is basically a tube like structure that leads to the chest cavity. Here, the trachea splits into two small tubes. These are called the *bronchi*. Each bronchus further divides into various *bronchial tubes*. It is

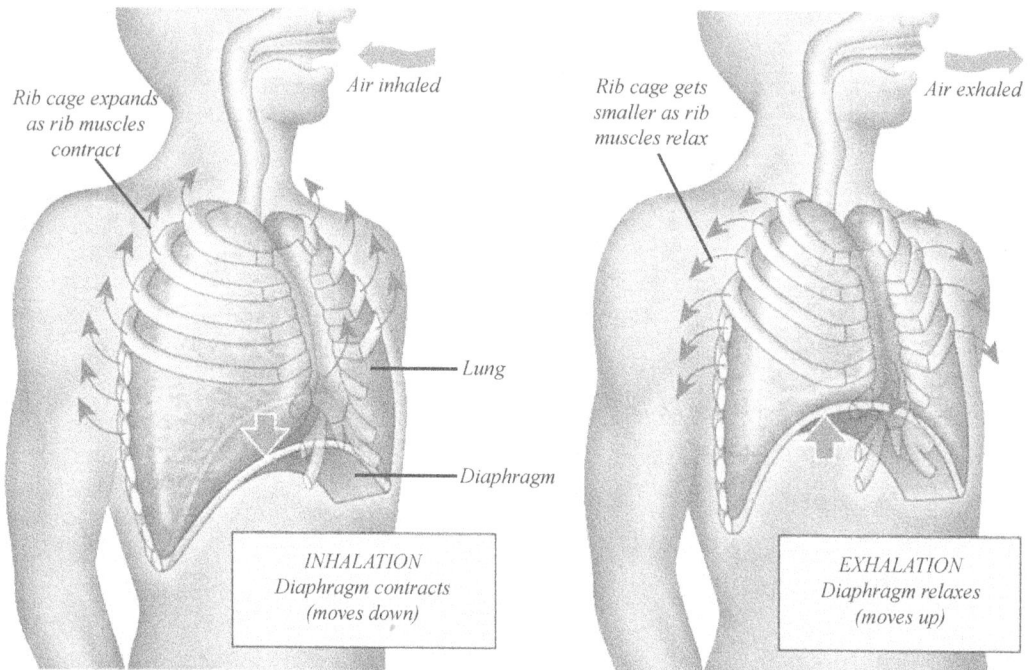

Rib cage expands as rib muscles contract

Air inhaled

Rib cage gets smaller as rib muscles relax

Air exhaled

Lung

Diaphragm

INHALATION
Diaphragm contracts
(moves down)

EXHALATION
Diaphragm relaxes
(moves up)

The Process of Inhaling Oxygen and Exhaling Carbon Dioxide in the Human Body

these bronchial tubes that lead directly into the lungs. They then divide into several smaller tubes which are connected to tiny sacs called the *alveoli*. It is an interesting fact that an average adult's lungs contain about 600 million of these spongy, air-filled sacs. The alveoli are surrounded by *capillaries*.

The oxygen we inhale passes into the alveoli, where it diffuses into the arterial blood, through the capillaries. During this time, the waste-rich blood from the veins releases its carbon dioxide into the alveoli. This carbon dioxide then goes out of the body through the same path, when we exhale.

It is the job of the *diaphragm* to help pump out the carbon dioxide from the lungs and pull oxygen into the body. The diaphragm is like a sheet of muscles, lying across the bottom of the chest cavity. The

process of breathing occurs as the *contraction* and *expansion* of the diaphragm occurs. At the time of contraction, oxygen is pulled into the lungs. On the other hand, when the diaphragm relaxes, carbon dioxide is pumped out of the lungs.

Together all these parts perform to ensure that the blood is circulated through out the body and hence, the *cells are supplied with adequate amount of oxygen* to make life possible on this Earth.

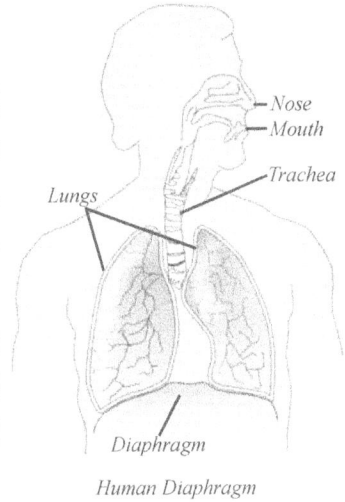

Nose
Mouth
Trachea
Lungs
Diaphragm

Human Diaphragm

Quick Facts

- We breathe around 6.5 litres of air each minute.
- There are 1500 miles of airways in the human respiratory system.
- The right lung is slightly larger than the left.
- Hairs in the nose help to clean the air we breathe as well as make it warm.
- The highest recorded "sneeze speed" is 165 km per hour.
- The surface area of the lungs is roughly of the same size as a tennis court.
- The capillaries in the lungs would extend to 1,600 km if placed end to end.
- We lose half a litre of water a day through breathing. This is the water vapour we see when we breathe onto glass.
- A person at rest usually breathes between 12 and 15 times a minute.
- The breathing rate is faster in children and women than in men.

Chapter - 2

THE EXCRETORY SYSTEM

The job of the excretory system is to remove waste products from the body. It removes both solid wastes and fluids. The parts of the excretory system are:

- **The kidneys**: *It filters and takes the waste out of the blood, and makes urine.*

The main organs of this system are:

- **The ureters**: *These are tubes that carry the urine to the bladder.*

- **The bladder**: *It is a bag like structure that collects the urine.*

- **The urethra**: *This is a tube that carries the urine out of the body.*

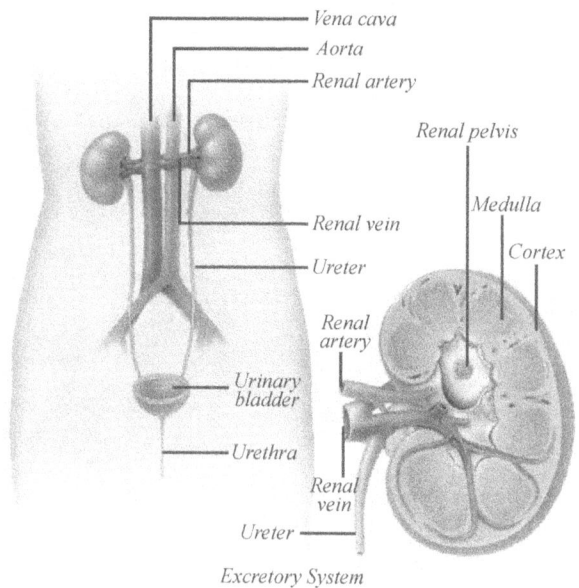

Excretory System

Functions of the Kidneys

One of the main jobs of the kidneys is to filter the waste out of the blood. These waste products may be a result of chemical reactions which occur from the breaking down of nutrients in our body. They may also be something which the body doesn't require because it already has enough of it. All these waste products have to be thrown out. That is the *excretory system's* responsibility.

How is it Cleaned up?

First, the blood is carried into the kidneys by the *renal artery* (anything in the body related to the kidneys is called "renal"). The kidney filters this blood about 400 times in a day. More than a million tiny filters called *nephrons* remove the waste products.

The waste that is collected combines with water (which is also filtered out of the kidneys) to make *urine*. As each kidney makes urine, the urine slides down a long tube called the *ureter* and collects in the *bladder*, a storage sac that holds the urine. When the bladder is about halfway full, your body tells you to go to the bathroom. When you pee, the urine goes from the bladder down another tube called the *urethra* and out of your body.

The kidneys also balance the volume of fluids and minerals in the body. This balance is called *homeostasis*. If you don't have enough fluids in your body, the brain communicates with the kidneys by sending out a hormone that tells the kidneys to hold on to some fluids. When you drink more, this hormone level goes down, and the kidneys will let go of more fluids.

The kidneys constantly react to the hormones that the brain sends them. The kidneys even make some of their own hormones. For example, the kidneys produce a hormone that tells the body to make the Red Blood Cells (RBCs).

Problems of the Kidneys

The kidneys are extremely vital organs. While there are many diseases of the excretory system, even more problems can be created by a malfunctioning set of kidneys. **Blood pressure** is closely tied to the amount of fluid in your body. If a kidney does not work and filter properly, blood pressure can increase to dangerous levels. Also, **urea** would accumulate in your tissues and would slowly poison the cells of your body.

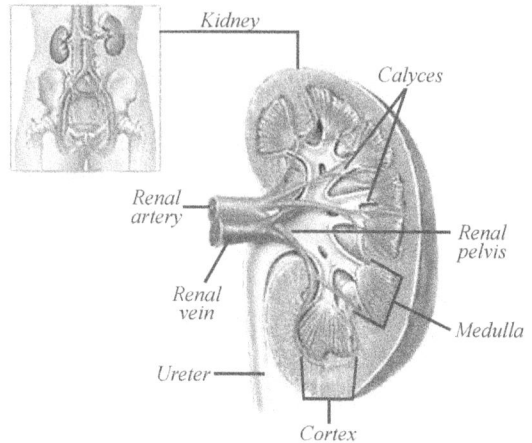

People with malfunctioning kidneys often have to go through a process called **dialysis**, where they are hooked up to a machine that filters their blood. The machine acts as an artificial kidney and tries to re-establish the normal levels of ions and water in their bodies.

Quick Facts

- When your urinary bladder is full, it is large enough to be noticeable, and when the urinary bladder is almost half full, the person discharges urine.

- Approximately 75 percent of human waste is made of water.

- The average person expels flatulence 14 times each day.

- Skin is not a part of the excretory system.

- Bladder cancer forms when cells lining the urinary bladder are abnormal.

- Kidney stones can move through your body.

- Kidney cancer forms when cells in the tissues of the kidney are abnormal.

- Kidney stones can be of the size of golf balls.
- Kidney stones are most common among white males over the age of 30.
- Most common symptoms in kidney cancer is blood in the urine.
- The colour of the urine is pale straw or amber.
- Water forms about 95 percent of the urine.
- Nephrones are urine forming structures of the kidneys.

Chapter - 3

THE DIGESTIVE SYSTEM

The human digestive system is responsible for breaking down the food we consume into smaller molecules that are usable by the body to obtain *energy and nutrition*. A very complex process, digestion consists of various organs, such as the *intestines, stomach*, etc., most of which are *tubular* in shape.

The process of digestion starts from the *mouth*. In the mouth, food is partially broken down by chewing with the help of certain chemical action of the *salivary enzymes*. These enzymes are produced by the *salivary glands* and are responsible for breaking down starches into smaller molecules.

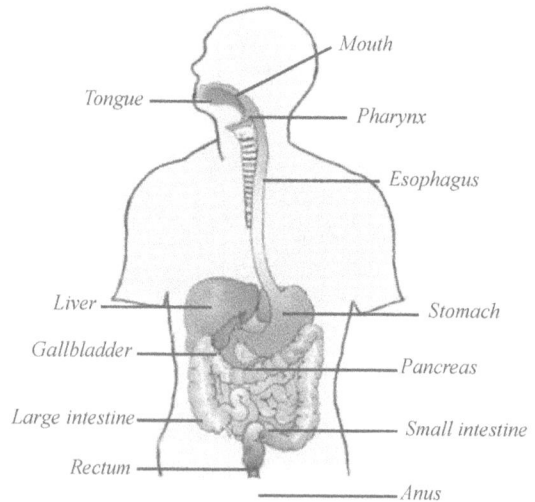

Digestive System

From the mouth, the chewed and swallowed food travels to the stomach through the *esophagus*, which is a long tube that runs from the mouth to the stomach. The esophagus uses coordinated, wave-like muscle movements to move food from the throat to the stomach. This rhythmic movement of the esophagus is called the *peristaltic*

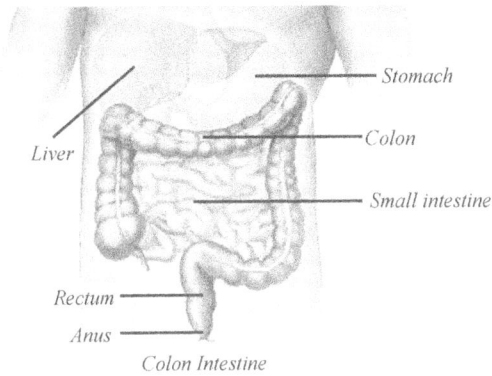

Colon Intestine

movement. The movement of this muscle gives us the ability to eat or drink even when we're upside-down!

Once the food reaches the stomach which is a huge, sack-like organ, the food is churned and gets bathed in a very strong

acid, called the *gastric acid*, which is basically the *Hydrochloric acid*. Food in the stomach that is partly digested and mixed with stomach acids is called the *chyme*.

The food then travels to the small intestine. Here, it enters the *duodenum*, which is the first part of the small intestine. It then

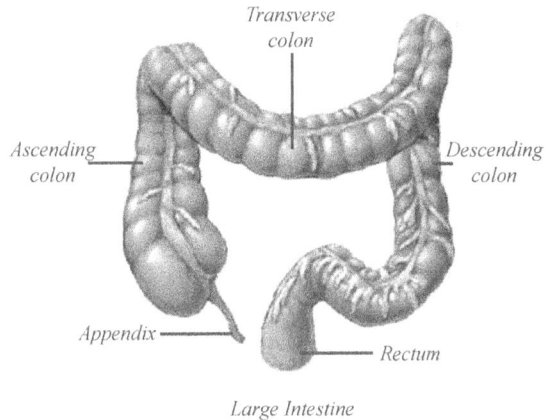

Large Intestine

goes on to the *jejunum* and then the *ileum*, which are the final parts of the small intestine. At this stage, the bile juice produced in the liver and the pancreatic enzymes, along with the other digestive enzymes produced by the inner wall of the small intestine assist in further breakdown of the food.

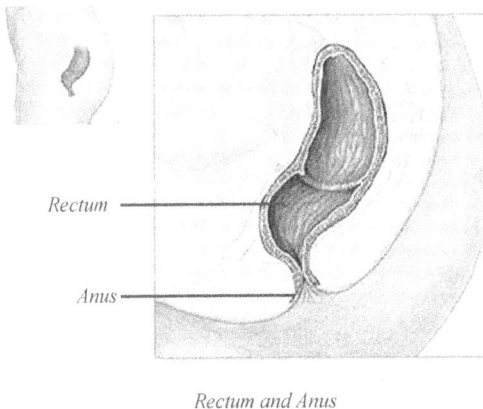

Rectum and Anus

After the small intestine, the food travels to the large intestine. Here, some of the water and chemicals like sodium, etc. are filtered out from the food. Various microbes (bacteria like Bacteroides, Escherichia coli, and Klebsiella) present in the large intestine also play a role in the digestion process. The first part of the large intestine is called the *cecum* or *caecum*, to which the *appendix* is connected. The remaining part of food then moves in an upward direction to the *ascending colon*. It then travels across the abdomen, through the transverse colon, goes back down the other side of the body in the *descending colon*, and then through the *sigmoid colon*.

The process of digestion then ends as the solid waste, which is stored in the *rectum*, is ejected out through the *anus*.

Quick Facts

- One can live without one's appendix.
- The food stays in our colon for 10 hours or for several days.
- We eat about 500kg of food per year and about 1.7 litres of saliva is produced each day.
- Our stomach can hold up to 1.5 litres of water or liquid material.
- One of the main functions of the mouth is to either cool or warm food to a neutral temperature acceptable for the rest of the digestive tract.
- An adult's stomach can hold approximately 1 litre of food, and it can expand four times its normal volume.
- The Small Intestine is at least 20 feet long.
- The Large Intestine is much shorter than the Small Intestine. It is approximately 5 feet long. The designation of "small" and "large" has to do with the width of the tube.

Chapter - 4

THE NERVOUS SYSTEM

The brain is the central organ that controls all the bodily functions. The nervous system is like a network that sends messages back and forth from the brain to different parts of the body. It does this via the spinal cord, which runs from the brain down through the back and contains

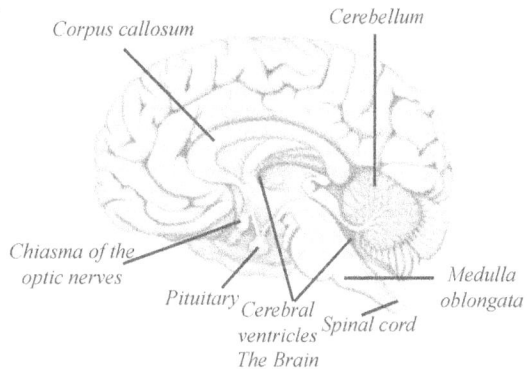

Corpus callosum
Cerebellum
Chiasma of the optic nerves
Pituitary
Cerebral ventricles
Spinal cord
Medulla oblongata
The Brain

threadlike nerves that are connected to every organ and body part.

When a message comes into the brain from anywhere in the body, the brain tells the body how to react. For example, if you accidentally touch a hot stove, the nerves in your skin shoot a message of pain to your brain. The brain then sends a message back telling the muscles in your hand to pull away. All this happens within a very short period of time.

The nervous system is divided into two kinds of systems:

The Central Nervous System

The Central Nervous System (CNS) is the processing centre for the nervous system. It receives information from and sends information to the Peripheral Nervous System. The two main organs of the CNS are the **brain** and the **spinal cord**. The human brain weighs just **3 pounds**. It has many folds and grooves which provide it with the additional surface area necessary for storing all of the body's important information.

The **spinal cord** is a long bundle of nerve tissues about 18 inches long and ¾ inch thick. It extends from the lower part of the brain down through the spine. The spinal cord is protected by a set of ring-shaped bones called the **vertebrae**.

They're cushioned by layers of membranes called the *meninges* and a special fluid called the **cerebrospinal fluid**. This fluid helps to protect the nerve tissues, keep it healthy, and remove the waste products.

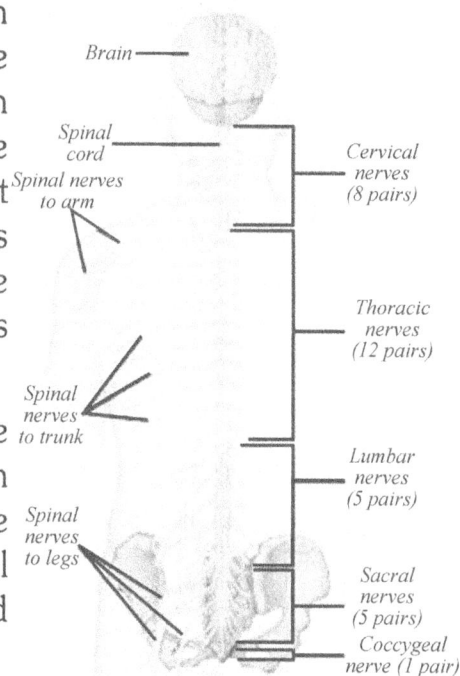

Brain

Spinal cord

Spinal nerves to arm

Spinal nerves to trunk

Spinal nerves to legs

Cervical nerves (8 pairs)

Thoracic nerves (12 pairs)

Lumbar nerves (5 pairs)

Sacral nerves (5 pairs)

Coccygeal nerve (1 pair)

Central Nervous System

The Peripheral Nervous System

Various nerves branch out from the spinal cord to the entire body. These are together called the Peripheral Nervous System.

The functioning of the nervous system depends on tiny cells called the **neurons**. The brain has a huge number of neurons, and all of them have specialised jobs. All the neurons send information and messages to each other through a *complex electrochemical process* that creates connections which affect the way our body functions. There are mainly two kinds of neurons, the **sensory** and the **motor neurons**.

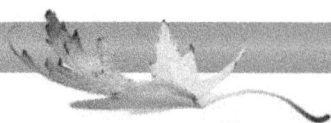

The Sensory Neurons send information from the Sensory Receptors (e.g., in skin, eyes, nose, tongue, ears, etc) towards the Central Nervous System.

The Motor Neurons send information from the central nervous system to the muscles or glands.

The Peripheral Nervous System is connected with various organs and structures of the body through **cranial nerves** and **spinal nerves**. There are *12 pairs of cranial nerves* in the brain that have connections in the head and upper body, and *31 pairs of spinal nerves* are connected to the rest of the body. While some cranial nerves contain only sensory neurons, most cranial nerves and all spinal nerves contain both motor and sensory neurons.

At the time of birth, the nervous system contains all the neurons we have, but all of them are not connected to each other. As you grow and learn, messages travel from one neuron to the other, thereby creating connections. For instance, a certain task may seem hard to perform in the beginning, but after you get used to, it becomes a part of you. This happens because a connection has now been made between the neurons.

Peripheral Nervous System Divisions:

- **Sensory Nervous System:** It sends information to the Central Nervous System (CNS) from our internal body organs or from the external stimuli.

- **Motor Nervous System:** This carries information from the CNS to the different organs, muscles and glands.

- **Somatic Nervous System:** It controls the skeletal muscles as well as the external sensory organs, such as the eyes, nose, ears, etc.

- **Autonomic Nervous System:** This controls the involuntary muscles, such as the smooth and the cardiac muscles.

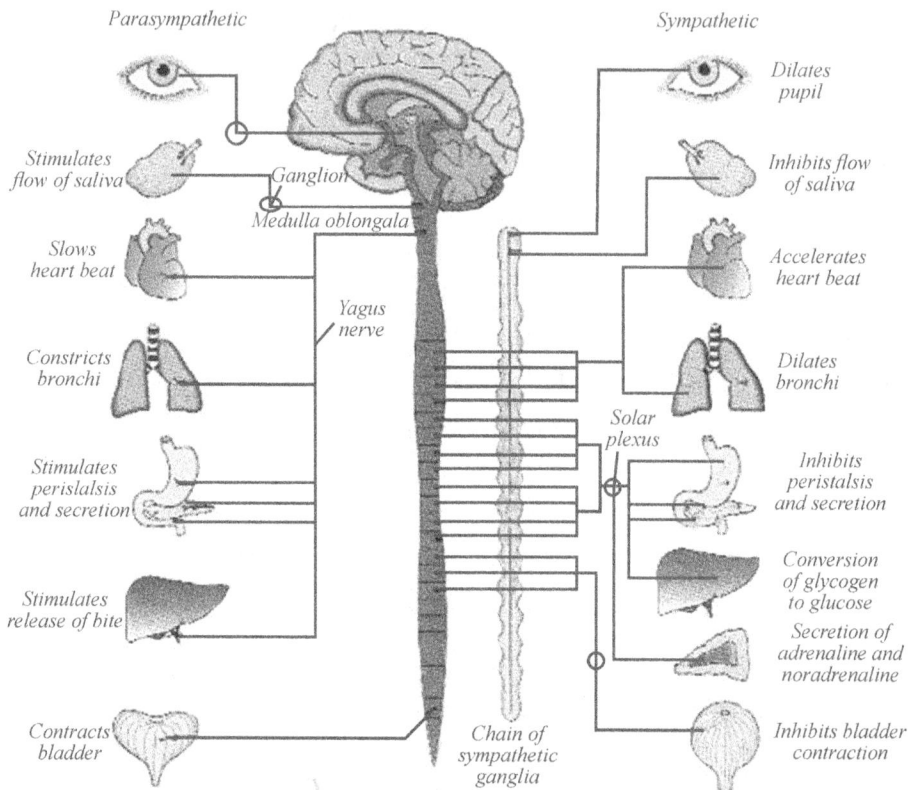

Parasympathetic / Sympathetic

Dilates pupil
Stimulates flow of saliva
Ganglion
Medulla oblongala
Inhibits flow of saliva
Slows heart beat
Yagus nerve
Accelerates heart beat
Constricts bronchi
Dilates bronchi
Solar plexus
Stimulates perislalsis and secretion
Inhibits peristalsis and secretion
Conversion of glycogen to glucose
Stimulates release of bile
Secretion of adrenaline and noradrenaline
Contracts bladder
Chain of sympathetic ganglia
Inhibits bladder contraction

Peripheral Nervous System

🎇 **Sympathetic System:** It controls activities that require high amounts of energy. It prepares the body for any kind of sudden stress or tension.

🎇 **Parasympathetic System:** It controls activities that conserve the body's energy and help it to rest.

Quick Facts

- **The human brain cell can hold five times as much information as the Encyclopedia Britannica.**
- **Nerve impulses to and from the brain travel as fast as 170 miles per hour.**

- In humans, the right side of the brain controls the left side of the body, while the left side of the brain controls the right side.
- There are millions of nerve cells in the human body. This number even exceeds the number of stars in the Milky Way.
  - The diameter of the neurons can range between 4 to 100 microns.
  - In a child developing inside the womb, neurons grow at the rate of 250,000 neurons per minute.
  - By the time of its birth, the baby's brain consists of around 10 million nerve cells or neurons.
  - The weight of the brain in average adult males is about 1375 grams, while in females, it is around1275 grams, and as we grow older, the brain loses a gram each year.
  - At a given point of time, only 4 percent of the cells in the brain are active, the rest are kept in reserve.

Chapter - 5

THE HEART AND THE CIRCULATORY SYSTEM

The heart is actually a muscle, which is located to the left of the middle of the chest. The size of the heart is about the same size of a fist.

The heart is a very special kind of muscle. Its job is to send blood all over the body. The heart and the circulatory system (also called the **cardiovascular system**)

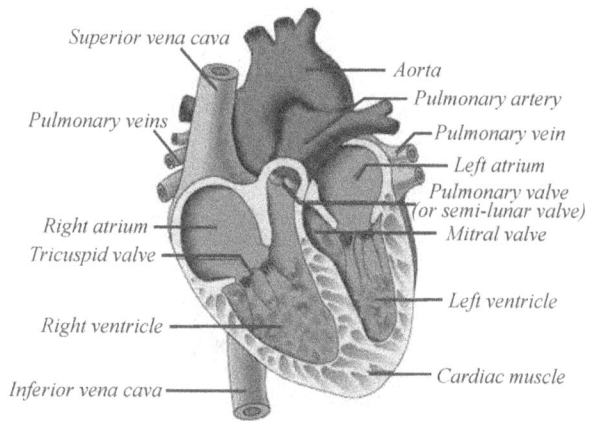

Superior vena cava
Aorta
Pulmonary artery
Pulmonary veins
Pulmonary vein
Left atrium
Pulmonary valve (or semi-lunar valve)
Right atrium
Mitral valve
Tricuspid valve
Right ventricle
Left ventricle
Inferior vena cava
Cardiac muscle

The Heart

make up the network that delivers blood to the body's tissues. With each heartbeat, blood is sent throughout our bodies, carrying oxygen and nutrients to all of our cells and also carrying away waste products. Our heart is like a **pump**. There are two sides of the heart. The left side receives blood from the lungs and pumps it to the rest of the body. The right side does the opposite. It receives blood from the various organs of the body and pumps it to the lungs. The heart fills with blood before each beat. Then its muscles contract to squirt the blood ahead.

Parts of the Heart

The heart is made of four different blood-filled areas called chambers. There are two chambers on each side of the heart. The top two chambers are called the **atria**. The atria fill with the blood returning to the heart from the body and the lungs. The heart has a left atrium and a *right atrium*. The bottom two chambers are called the *ventricles*. The heart has a *left ventricle* and a *right ventricle*. Their job is to send blood to the body and the lungs. Running down the middle of the heart is a thick wall of muscle called the *septum*. Its job is to separate the left and right side of the heart.

How the System Works

The *atria* and the *ventricles* work together- the atria fill with blood, and then send it to the ventricles. The ventricles then squeeze, pumping blood out of the heart.

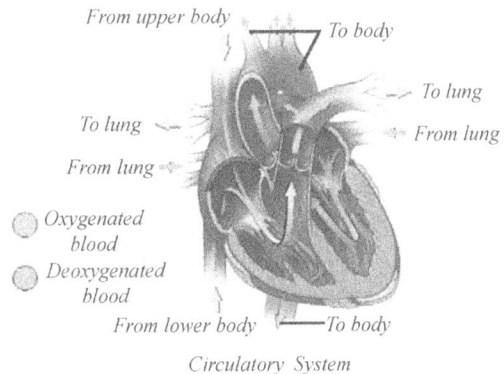

From upper body
To body
To lung
To lung
From lung
From lung
Oxygenated blood
Deoxygenated blood
From lower body
To body

Circulatory System

While the ventricles are squeezing, the atria refill and get ready for the next contraction.

Blood circulates on *four valves inside the heart*. Two of the heart valves are the *mitral valves* and the other two are the *tricuspid valves*. They let blood flow from the atria to the ventricles. The other two are called the *aortic valve* and the *pulmonary valve*, and they're in charge of controlling the flow as the blood leaves the heart. These valves all work to keep the blood flowing forward. They open up to let the blood move ahead, and then they close quickly to keep the blood from flowing backward.

The blood moves around in our body through a series of tubes called the **arteries** and **veins**, which are collectively called the *blood vessels*. These blood vessels are attached to the heart. The blood vessels that carry blood away from the heart are called the arteries. The ones that carry blood back to the heart are called the veins. This whole system is called the **circulatory system**, and this is our body's lifeline.

The movement of the blood through the heart and around the body is called circulation. The heart takes *less than 60 seconds* to pump blood to every cell in our body. Blood delivers oxygen to all the body's cells. To stay alive, a person needs healthy, living cells. Without oxygen, these cells would die. If that oxygen-rich blood doesn't circulate as it should, a person could die. The left side of your heart sends that oxygen-rich blood out to the body. The body takes the oxygen out of the blood and uses it in your body's cells. When the cells use the oxygen, they make carbon dioxide and other waste products that get carried away by the blood.

The returning blood enters the right side of the heart. The right ventricle pumps the blood to the lungs for a little freshening up. In the lungs, carbon dioxide is removed from the blood and sent out of the body when we **exhale**. After we **inhale**, the whole process starts again. All this happens in less than a minute.

Pulse

A way to know that the heart is working, from the outside, is to feel our pulse. We can find our pulse by lightly pressing on the skin anywhere there's a large artery running just beneath our skin. Two good places to find it are on the side of our neck and the inside of our wrist, just below the

Heart Beats (Pulse)

thumb. When we feel a small beat under our skin, that is when we have found our pulse. Each beat is caused by the contraction of the heart. An adult normal human heart beats about **72 times per minute**.

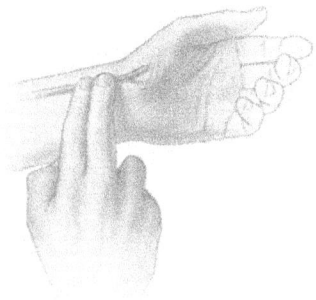

Quick Facts

- The human heart creates enough pressure to squirt blood to about 30 feet.

- The human body is estimated to have 60,000 miles of blood vessels.

- Simple and moderately severe sunburn damages the blood vessels extensively.

- A woman's heart beats faster than a man's heart. The main reason for this is simply that on average, women tend to be smaller than men and have less mass to pump blood to.

- The aorta is the largest artery of the human body. All the arteries carry the blood out of your heart.

- Veins carry the blood back to the heart.

- If your blood vessels were strung together and measured, they would circle the globe 2 1/2 times.

- In just one to two minutes, blood circulates throughout your whole body. It brings the oxygen out and the carbon dioxide back within that short amount of time, and then it repeats, and repeats and repeats your whole life.

Chapter - 6

NUTRITION

Human body is extremely complex in nature and hence, requires energy to function and nutrients to grow and repair any damage in the system. These nutrients and energy come from food. Therefore, the consumption of a good balanced diet is essential.

Nutrition can be broadly categorised into three types of food – **carbohydrates, proteins** and **fats**. Apart from these major components, tiny amounts of **vitamins** and **minerals** are also required. Other key components include **water** and **fibre**. To stay in good shape, a person should eat a variety of food in adequate proportions.

The main source of energy for our body, i.e. the carbohydrates can be categorised into two parts – *Complex carbohydrates* and *Sweet-tasting sugars*.

- **Complex Carbohydrates:** The main complex carbohydrate in our body is starch. Pastas, cereals, bread, rice, potatoes, etc. are rich in starch. Such foods, containing complex carbohydrates should

constitute at least half of our diet, as during digestion, this starch is broken up into sugar glucose, which is the main source of energy for the body.

- **Sugars:** Foods containing this form of carbohydrates should be eaten sparingly as they contain a lot of added sugar. Sweets, cakes, biscuits, etc. contain sugar. These foods give the body a sudden energy burst rather than a constant stream. These foods also cause the problem of weight gain.

- **Proteins and Dairy Products:** Proteins and dairy products ensure the growth and development of the body. They also help in repairing the damaged parts of our system. Foods rich in proteins are fish, pulses, eggs, meat, nuts, etc. Dairy products enable healthy bone growth. For example, milk and cheese supply bone building mineral, called the calcium. These foods should constitute at least 15% of our diet.

- **Fats and Oils:** Fats and oils are responsible for providing vitamins that are essential for the smooth functioning of our body. However, they should be consumed in moderation as animal foods contain saturated fatty acids

which can clog the arteries. However, plant oils, such as olive oil, containing unsaturated fatty acids are good for health.

- **Fruits and Vegetables:** These are the most essential parts of a diet and should be consumed in abundance. Fruits are a great source of fibre, water and minerals that give us energy and replenish our bodies. They also supply antioxidants which reduce the possibility of contracting diseases. Vegetables are also rich in fibre, and hence are a vital part of a balanced diet.

Quick Facts

- We can survive for months without food but only a few days without water.

- One tires easily due to lack of iron in the body.

- Water helps to regulate the body temperature. Water rids the body of waste materials and transports vital nutrients to the cells.

- Plants can manufacture most of the nutrients that they need to function but human beings cannot - humans must obtain nutrients by eating plants and animals.

Chapter - 7

IMMUNITY

The immune system of our body is like a *defence system* that protects us from all the foreign particles that enter it. It is a collection of molecules, cells and organs whose complex interactions form an efficient system that is usually able to protect an individual from both foreign invaders and its own internal cells. This way our body stays protected from infections and diseases.

Brain Tumour

The combination of these components has emerged after millions of years of evolution, which has targeted those species that are worthy of preventing their destruction from the attack of **micro-organisms** or **tumours**.

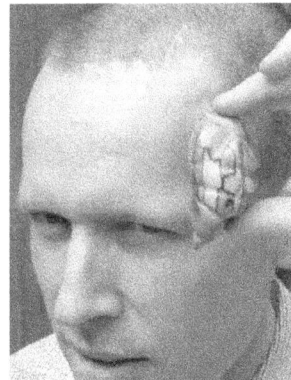

A very peculiar fact about the human immunity is that it works the most when it doesn't have to work at all, meaning at the time the body is not contracted by diseases. Therefore, if the infectious *bacteria* or *viruses* are unable to enter an individual's body, no further immune response will be needed. Hence, the person remains healthy.

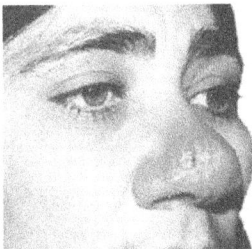

It is important to note that two other body parts that are not usually associated with the

immune system also serve vital functions. These are the **Skin** and the **Mucosa**. While it seems elementary, the importance of skin in resisting infection cannot be overlooked. It is the skin which stops most of the micro-organisms from entering the body, hence, protecting it against **diseases**. To appreciate its importance, it is important to consider the relative frequency of wounds or rashes forming on healthy skin, as compared to where the skin has been infected.

The other important feature is the Mucosa. It is the tissue which covers our eyes, alimentary canal, urinary and genital tracts. If the frequency of infections at these areas is high, it gets difficult for the tissue to resist them. It is lesser efficient than the skin in this job as it is easier to penetrate this tissue.

Tears and saliva, as well as other mucus secretions perform the job of washing away many potential attackers, and many also contain chemical elements which are effective in killing microbes.

The cells that serve the Immune system are known as the **B-Cells** and the **T-Cells**. The T-Cells act to destroy the infected or cancerous cells, and also coordinate all the acquired immune responses. The T-Cell immunity is generally called the *cellular immunity*.

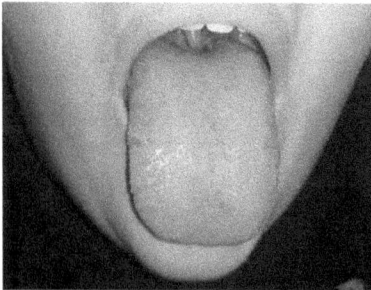

On the other hand, the B-Cells provide humoral immunity as it consists of dissolved proteins found in the 'Humors' (Blood).

Quick Facts

- Increasing stress leads to decreasing immunity.

- We get an allergy when the immune system responds to a harmless substance.

- Coughing and sneezing are part of the natural immunity system where the body is trying to eject pathogens and irritants from the respiratory system.

- Saliva, tears and breast milk contain antibacterial enzymes to help fight off harmful bacteria.

- One of the first responses to infection by the immune system is inflammation.

- Fever can sometimes help the immune system fight off infection because certain pathogens are unable to tolerate higher temperatures.

- The lungs and intestines secrete mucus, which can trap micro-organisms, preventing them from entering the bloodstream and tissues.

- The gastric acid produced by the stomach not only aids in digestion but is also a chemical barrier that destroys many forms of ingested pathogens.

Part - III

THE EXTERNAL ORGANS

Chapter - 1

MOUTH

The mouth plays a key role in the **digestive system**, but it does much more than get digestion started. The mouth - especially the teeth, lips, and tongue - is essential for speech. The tongue, which allows us to taste, also helps form words when we speak. The lips that line the outside of the mouth both help hold food in while we chew and pronounce words when we talk.

Along with the lips and tongue, the teeth help to form words by controlling air flow out of the mouth. The tongue strikes the teeth as certain sounds are made.

The hardest substances in the body, the teeth are also necessary for *chewing* - the process by which we tear, cut, and grind food in preparation for swallowing. Chewing allows enzymes and lubricants released in the mouth to further digest food.

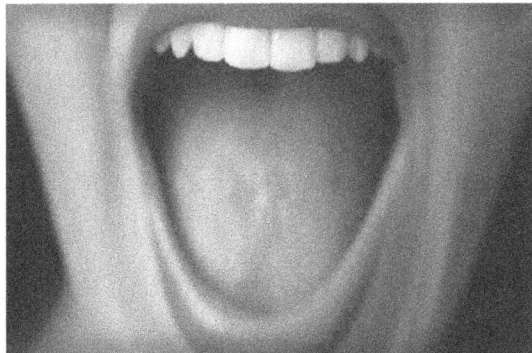

Mouth

The mouth is the entrance to the digestive tract, and is lined with *mucus membranes*. The roof of the mouth is called the *palate*. The front part consists of a bony portion called the *hard palate*, with a fleshy rear part called the *soft palate*. The hard palate divides the mouth and the nasal passages above. The soft palate forms a curtain between the mouth and the throat, or pharynx, to the rear. The soft palate contains the *uvula*, the dangling flesh at the back of the mouth. The *tonsils* are located on either side of the uvula. They hold up the opening to the pharynx.

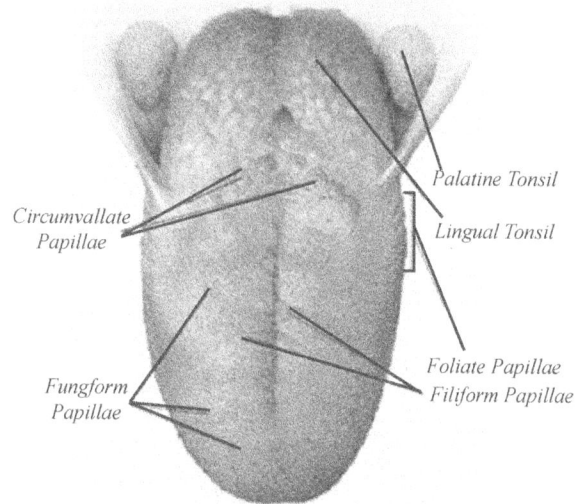

Circumvallate Papillae

Fungform Papillae

Palatine Tonsil

Lingual Tonsil

Foliate Papillae
Filiform Papillae

Part of the Tongue

A bundle of muscles extends from the floor of the mouth to form the tongue. The upper surface of the tongue is covered with tiny bumps called the *papillae*. These contain tiny pores that are our *taste buds*. Four main kinds of taste buds are found on the tongue — those that sense sweet, salty, sour, and bitter tastes. Three pairs of salivary glands secrete saliva, which contains a digestive enzyme called *amylase* that starts the breakdown of carbohydrates even before food enters the stomach.

The lips are covered with skin on the outside and with slippery mucous membranes on the inside of the mouth. The major lip muscle, called the *orbicularis oris*, allows for the lips' mobility. The reddish tint of the lips comes from the underlying blood vessels. The inside portion of both the lips is connected to the *gums*.

There are several types of teeth. **Incisors** are squarish, sharp-edged teeth in the front of the mouth. There are four on the bottom and four on the top. On either side of the incisors are the sharp canines. Behind the **canines** are the **premolars**, or **bicuspids**. There are two sets in each jaw. The molars, situated behind the premolars, have points and grooves. There are 12 molars — three sets in each jaw called the first, second, and the third molars.

Human teeth are made up of four different types of tissue: *pulp, dentin, enamel, and cementum*. The pulp is the innermost portion of the tooth and consists of the connective tissue, nerves and blood vessels, which nourish the tooth. **Dentin** surrounds the pulp. A hard yellow substance, and it makes up most of the tooth and is as hard as the bone. It's the dentin that gives teeth their yellowish tint.

Enamel, the hardest tissue in the body, covers the dentin and forms the outermost layer of the crown. It enables the tooth to withstand the pressure of chewing and protects it from harmful bacteria. It also helps to withstand changes in the temperature from hot and cold foods. Both the dentin and pulp extend into the roots of the teeth. A bony layer of cementum covers the outside of the root, under the gum line, and holds the tooth in place within the jawbone. **Cementum** is also as hard as the bone.

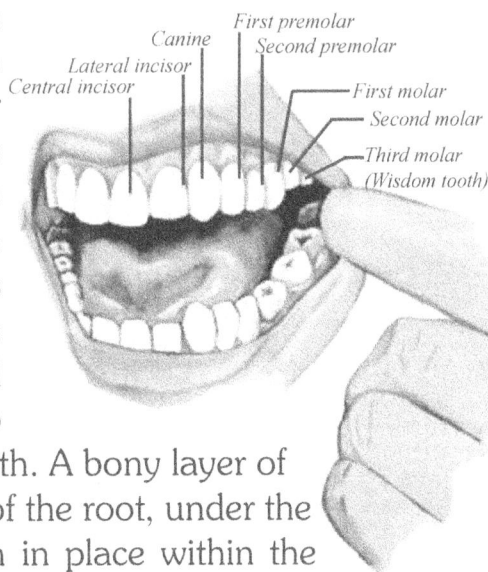

Central incisor
Lateral incisor
Canine
First premolar
Second premolar
First molar
Second molar
Third molar
(Wisdom tooth)

Types of Teeth

What the mouth and teeth do?

The first step of digestion involves the mouth and teeth. Food enters the mouth and is immediately broken down into smaller pieces by our teeth. Each type of tooth serves a different function in the chewing process. **Incisors** cut foods when you bite into them. The

sharper and longer **canines** tear food. The **premolars**, which are flatter than the canines, grind and mash food. **Molars**, with their

points and grooves, are responsible for the most vigorous chewing. The tongue helps to push the food up against our teeth.While chewing, the salivary glands secrete saliva, which moistens the food and helps break it down even more. Saliva makes it easier to chew and swallow foods and it contains enzymes that aid in the digestion.

Once food has been converted into a soft, moist mass, it's pushed into the throat (or pharynx) at the back of the mouth and is swallowed. When we swallow, the soft palate closes off the nasal passages from the throat to prevent food from entering the nose.

Proper dental care - including a good diet, frequent cleaning of the teeth after eating, and regular dental checkups - all these are essential in maintaining healthy teeth and avoiding tooth decay and gum diseases.

Quick Facts

- **If saliva cannot dissolve something, you cannot taste it.**
- **The tooth is the only part of the human body that can't repair itself.**
- **Throughout your life, the amount of saliva you have could fill two swimming pools.**
- **If your mouth was completely dry, you would not be able to distinguish the taste of anything.**
- **Humans have unique tongue prints, just like fingerprints.**
- **The tongue is the strongest muscle in the body.**

Chapter - 2

EARS

We hear many different sounds all around us. The body parts that help us with this are the ears.

The ears collect sounds, process them, and send sound signals to your brain. Also, our ears help us keep our balance, which means that they help us in standing straight and not falling down.

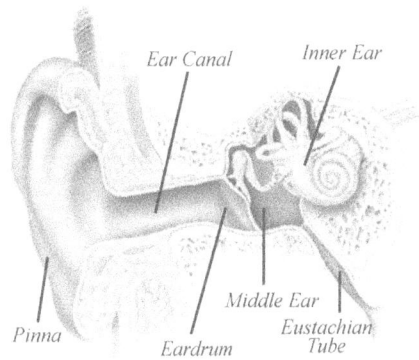

Parts of Human Ear

Parts of the Ear

The ear has three different sections:

- *Outer Ear:* *This part is also called the pinna or auricle. This is the part of the ear that can be seen. The outer ear hears and collects sounds. The outer ear also includes the ear canal, the place where the earwax is produced. Earwax protects the ear canal. It contains chemicals that fight infections that may hurt the skin in the canal. It also collects dirt to help keep the ear canal clean.*

- *Middle Ear:* *Sound waves, after entering the ear, travel through the ear canal to the middle ear. The middle ear's* main job is to take these sound waves and turn them into vibrations, which are then sent to the inner ear. To do this, it needs the eardrum, a thin piece of skin which is stretched tight to seem like a drum. When sound waves reach the ear drum, it vibrates. The sound then moves to the ossicles, which are three tiny bones in our ear. These are called the

- **Hammer:** which is attached to the ear drum
- **Anvil:** which is attached to the hammer, and
- **Stirrup:** which is attached to the anvil, and is also the smallest bone in the body. These bones help the sound waves in moving to the inner ear.
- **Inner Ear:** Sounds enter the inner ear in the form of vibrations, and from there enter the cochlea which is a small, curled tube. The cochlea is filled with liquid, which is set into motion when the ossicles vibrate. The cochlea is lined with tiny cells covered with tiny hairs.
- **The Cochlea:** The sounds move the hair on the cells, creating nerve signals for the brain.

The brain then recognises the various sounds that it receives.

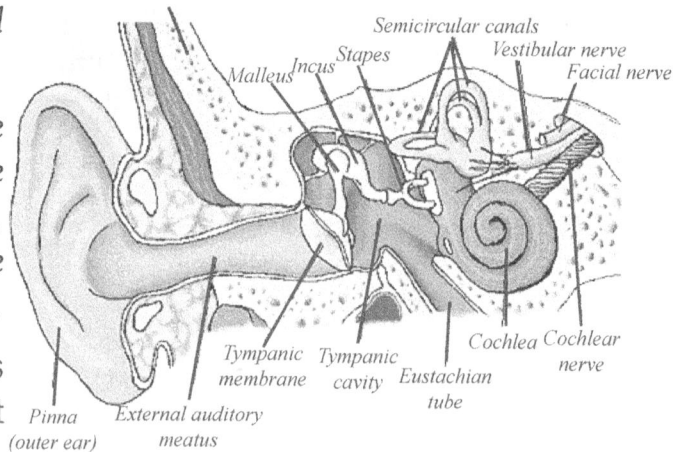

The Internal Structure of Human Ear

Maintaining Balance

Ears also help us maintain our balance. In the inner ear, there are three small loops above the cochlea called the **semicircular canals**. They are filled with liquid and have tiny microscopic hair, just like the cochlea. When we move our heads, the liquid moves too. The liquid moves the tiny hairs, which send a nerve message to the brain about the position of our heads. Within a second, the brain sends a message to the right muscles so that we can keep our balance.

Quick Facts

- Earwax production is necessary for good ear health.
- After eating too much, your hearing is less sharp.
- Your ears secrete more earwax when you are afraid than when you aren't.
- The smallest bone in your body, the stirrup, is in your ears.

Chapter - 3

EYES

The eyes are one of the most spectacular parts of the body because they let us view the world all around us. Except for when we are sleeping, our eyes are always working. They take in information from what we see in the world, and then send that information to our brain so that the brain knows what is happening around us.

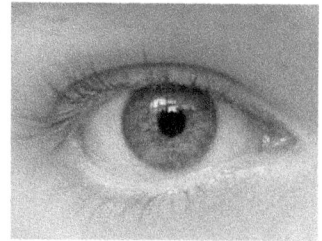

The Human Eye

Parts and Functions of the Eye

The eye rests in a hollow area called the **eye socket**, in the skull. The eyelid covers and protects the front part of the eyes. It also keeps the eye clean and moist by opening and closing several times. This action is called *blinking*. The eyelid also has amazing reflexes, in order to protect the eye. When we step into bright light, our eyelids instantly close to protect the eyes before they can adjust themselves to the light.

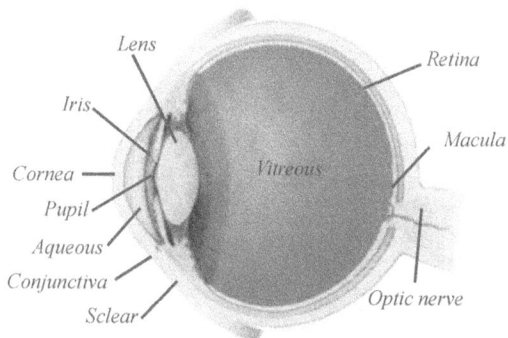

Parts of the Human Eye

The eyelashes are the hair that grow on the top and bottom of the eyelid and protect the *eyes* by keeping dust and other unwanted objects from entering the *eyes*.

The white part of the eyeball is called the **sclera**. It is made up of a tough material, and is like an outer coat of the eyeball. The pink and red threads that can be seen are **blood vessels**, and provide blood to the sclera.

The **cornea** is a transparent part which sits in front of the coloured part of the *eye*. The cornea helps the *eye* focus as light makes its way through. It is a very important part of the *eye*, and gives a clear and transparent view of the world around us.

The **iris**, the **pupil** and the **anterior chamber** lie behind the *cornea*. The iris is the coloured part of the *eye*. When we say that a person has brown eyes, we are actually referring to his/her iris. The iris has attached muscles that change its shape. These allow the iris to control the amount of light that enters the pupil.

The pupil is situated in the centre of the iris, and is like an opening through which light enters the *eye*. Pupils get smaller when a light is shone near them, and grow bigger when the light is dimmed or gone.

The anterior chamber is the space between the *iris* and the *cornea*. It is filled with a special transparent fluid that nourishes the *eye* and keeps it healthy.

After light enters the pupil, it reaches the *lens*. The lens is situated behind the iris and is clear and colourless.

The lens then focusses light rays to the back of the eyeball, that is, to the retina. The retina has millions of cells that are sensitive to light. The **retina** changes the *light into nerve signals* and sends them to the brain, so that the brain can understand what the *eye* is saying.

The *vitreous site behind the retina* is the biggest part of the eye. It gives the eye its shape. It's filled with clear and jelly-like material called the *vitreous humour*. After light passes through the lens, it shines through the vitreous humour to the back of the eye.

Rods and Cones

The retina uses *rods* and *cones* to process light. Rods see in black and white, and shades of grey. They tell us the form and shape of anything that we see. Rods don't know the difference between colours. But they are super-sensitive, and help us see in the dark. Cones sense colour, and unlike rods, are mostly helpful in normal or bright light. There are

Internal Structure of an Eye

three types of cones, each of which is sensitive to the three primary colours, that is, red, green and blue. This allows one to see different ranges of colour. When they work together, these cones can sense a combination of light waves that enable us to see many colours.

The rods and cones change the colours and shapes into *nerve messages*. These messages are then carried by the optic nerve to the brain. When we see an image, our eyes inform our brain about what they saw, and then the brain works to figure out what it is that the eyes see.

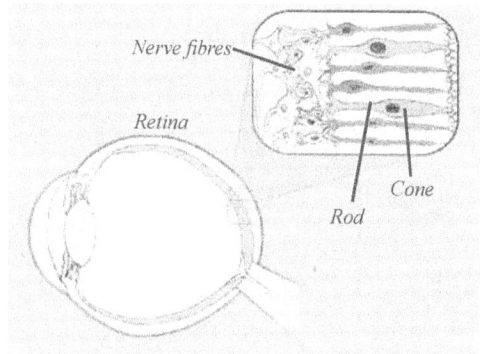

Lacrimal Glands (Tear glands)

The lacrimal glands are situated above the outer corner of each eye. These glands produce tears. Every time we blink, a little bit of tear fluid comes out of this gland. It helps wash away the dust, germs and anything else that might irritate the eyes. Tears also protect our eyes from drying out. Sometimes the eyes make more tear fluid to

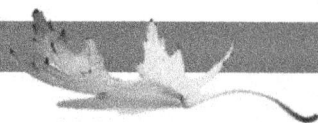

protect themselves. This can happen when we are poked in the eye, when we are in a very polluted place, or when we are cutting onions. Whenever we are sad or scared, the brain sends messages to the eyes to cry, and then the **lacrimal glands** make many **tears**.

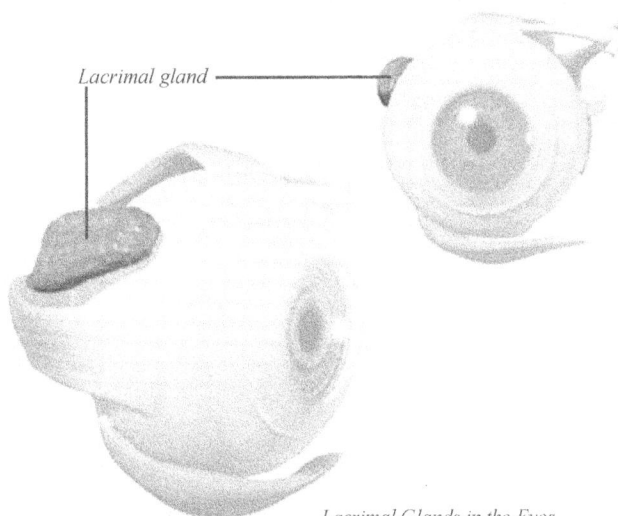

Lacrimal gland

Lacrimal Glands in the Eyes

Quick Facts

- Humans are the only animals to produce emotional tears.

- The pupils dilate both when you look at a person you love and at a person you hate. Even small noises cause the pupils of the eyes to dilate.

- Babies are always born with blue eyes because of the pigment, melanin. The melanin in a newborn's eyes often needs time after birth to be fully deposited or to be darkened by exposure to ultraviolet light, later revealing the baby's true eye colour.

- Eyes detect light and allow us to see.

- Our eyes blink over 27,397 times in a day.

- The eyeball of a human weighs approximately 28 grams.

- Cone cells in the retina detect colour while rod cells detect low light.

- Glasses and contact lenses are worn to correct common sight conditions, such as short and long-sightedness.

Chapter - 4

JOINTS

The place where two **bones meet** is called a joint. Some joints **move** and others **don't**.

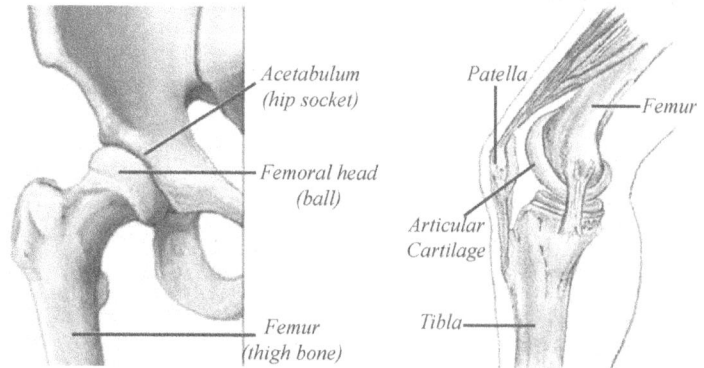

Acetabulum (hip socket)

Femoral head (ball)

Femur (thigh bone)

Patella

Femur

Articular Cartilage

Tibla

Joints of the Legs

Types of Joints

- ✹ **Fixed joints** are fixed in place and don't move at all. Your skull has some of these joints called *sutures* which close up the bones of the skull in a young person's head.

- ✹ **Moving joints** are the ones that allow you to twist, bend and move different parts of your body. Some moving joints, like the ones in your spine, move only a little. Other joints move a lot.

  - ☆ One of the main types of moving joints is called a **hinge joint**. Your elbows and knees each have hinge joints, which let you bend and then straighten your arms and legs. These joints are like the hinges on a door. Just as most doors can only open one way, you can only

bend your arms and legs in one direction. You also have many smaller hinge joints in your fingers and toes.

Pivot Joint

Ball-and-socket Joint

Hinge Joint

Ellipsoid Joint

Saddle Joint

Gliding Joint

Different Types of Joints

★ Another important type of moving joint is the **ball and socket joint**. You can find these joints at your shoulders and hips. They are made up of the round end of one bone fitting into a small cup-like area of another bone. Ball and socket joints allow for lots of movement in every direction.

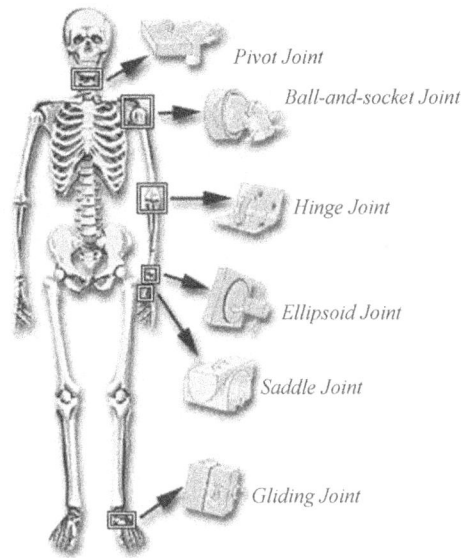

Your joints come with their own special fluid called the **synovial fluid** that helps them move freely. Bones are held together at the joints by ligaments, which are like very strong rubber bands.

Quick Facts

- Humans have over 230 moveable and semi-moveable joints in their bodies.

- Some joints move and some don't. Joints in the skull don't move.

- Synovial joints are movable joints. They make up most of the joints in the body and are located mostly in the limbs, where the mobility is critical. They contain synovial fluid, which helps them to move freely.

- A coating of another fibrous tissue called cartilage covers the bone surface and keeps the bones from rubbing directly against each other.

- Tendons are made of elastic tissue and also play a key role in the functioning of joints. They connect the muscles to the bones.

- Ball and socket joints, such as hip and shoulder joints, are the most mobile type of joints. They allow you to move your arms and legs in many different directions.

- Ellipsoidal joints, such as the one at the base of the index finger, allow bending and extending.

- Gliding joints are found between flat bones that are held together by ligaments. Some bones in the wrists and ankles move by gliding against each other.

- Hinge joints are those in the knee and elbow. They enable movement similar to the way a hinged door moves.

Chapter - 5

THE SKELETAL SYSTEM

The human skeleton is a strong and flexible framework, which not only supports the shape of the body, but also produces movements when pulled by the muscles. The human body consists of **206 bones**. It is also the job of the skeleton to protect the soft, internal organs, such as the brain and lungs. It may be interesting to know that bones, which make up about 20% of the body's mass, are connected to each other at joints and are held together by strong straps of tissue, called the **ligaments**.

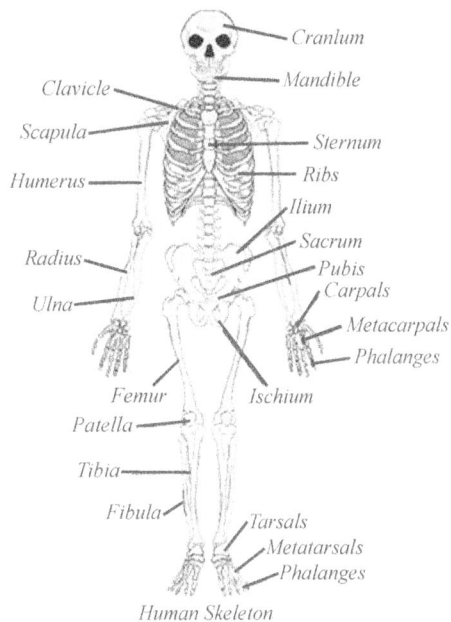

Human Skeleton

Skull

The bones in the skull are responsible for protecting the brain and provide a framework to the face. These also regulate the *facial expressions*.

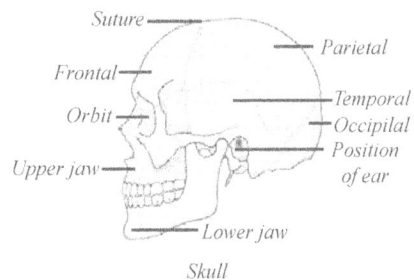

Skull

The skull consists of **22 bones**, 21 of which are locked together by **sutures**.

Chest

Chest is formed by the breastbone, ribs and part of the back bone. These bones together perform a protective cage to protect the lungs and the heart from any damage.

Forearm

Two parallel bones, the ulna and the radius together form the forearm. The ulna curves to form the elbow's point, whereas the radius forms a joint with the wrist bones.

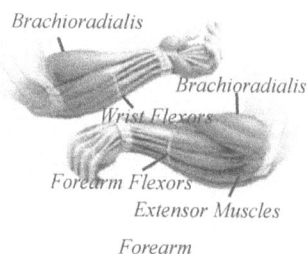

Brachioradialis
Brachioradialis
Wrist Flexors
Forearm Flexors
Extensor Muscles

Forearm

Elbow

Elbow is the point where the upper arm and the forearm meet. The elbow acts like a door hinge, enabling the arm to bend and keep straight. The forearm can rotate the elbow, allowing the palm to face upwards or downwards.

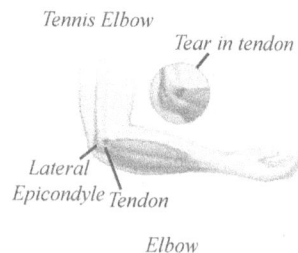

Tennis Elbow
Tear in tendon
Lateral Epicondyle
Tendon

Elbow

Knee

The knee is the joint between the shin and the thigh. It is the strongest and the most complex joint of the body. It allows the leg to bend and keep straight, and supports the body's weight during activities like running, walking, jumping, etc.

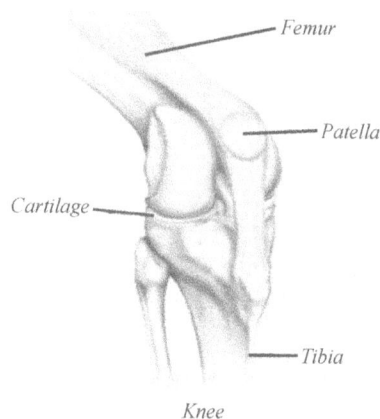

Femur
Patella
Cartilage
Tibia

Knee

Pelvis

This is a strong, bowl shaped structure consisting of two curved hip bones. It supports abdominal organs and attaches the thigh bones to the skeleton.

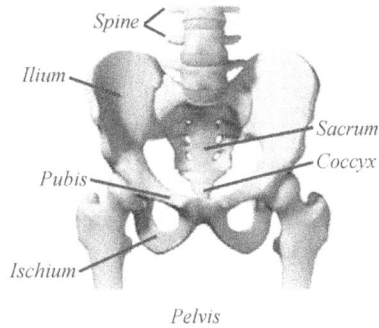

Spine

Ilium

Sacrum

Coccyx

Pubis

Ischium

Pelvis

Hand

The hand consists of **27 bones** and many movable joints that are responsible to perform very many tasks. The thumb can be rotated to touch each of the other fingers.

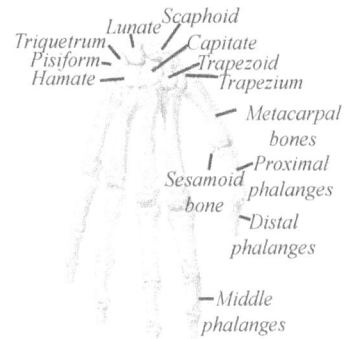

Lunate Scaphoid

Triquetrum Capitate

Pisiform Trapezoid

Hamate Trapezium

Metacarpal bones

Proximal phalanges

Sesamoid bone

Distal phalanges

Middle phalanges

Hand

Foot

A foot consists of the **ankle**, **sole** and the **toe bones** which support and move the body's weight. They provide a flexible platform to the body.

Toes

The **phalanges** of the toes are shorter than the phalanges of the hands and not as flexible as the ones in the fingers. These help the body to propel forward.

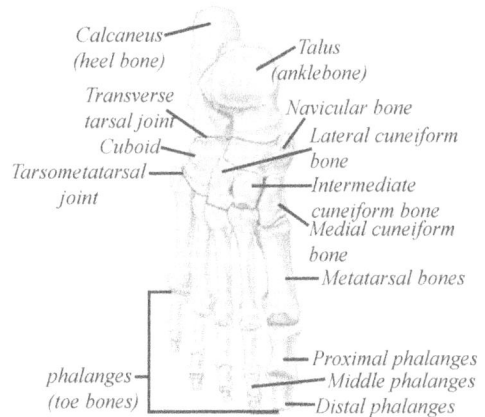

Calcaneus (heel bone)

Talus (anklebone)

Transverse tarsal joint

Navicular bone

Cuboid

Lateral cuneiform bone

Tarsometatarsal joint

Intermediate cuneiform bone

Medial cuneiform bone

Metatarsal bones

phalanges (toe bones)

Proximal phalanges

Middle phalanges

Distal phalanges

Foot and Toes

Backbone or the Spine

The spine, also known as the backbone or the **vertebral column**, consists of a long chain of **33 bones** each individually known as a *vertebra* or the *vertebrae*, which are ring-shaped. The main functions of the vertebral bones

are for structure and protection of the spinal cord. The spine lets you twist and bend, and it holds your body upright. It also protects the spinal cord, a large bundle of nerves that sends information from your brain to the rest of your body.

Backbone of the Spine

There are different types of vertebrae in the spine and each does a different kind of job:

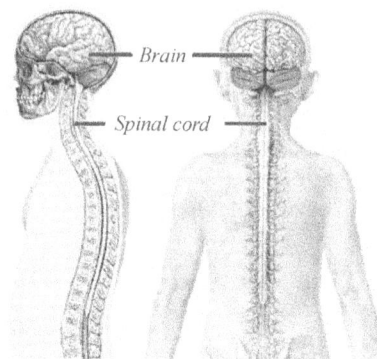

- The first seven vertebrae at the top are called the **cervical vertebrae**. These bones are the back of your neck, just below your brain, and they support your head and neck.

- Below the cervical vertebrae are the **thoracic vertebrae**, and they are 12 in all. These anchor your ribs in place.

- Below the thoracic vertebrae are five **lumbar vertebrae**.

- Beneath the lumbar vertebrae is the **sacrum**, which is made up of five vertebrae that are fused together to form one single bone.

- Finally, all the way at the bottom of the spine is the **coccyx**, which is one bone made of four fused vertebrae.

The bottom sections of the spine are important when it comes to bearing weight and giving you a good centre of gravity. So when you pick up a heavy bag on an object, the lumbar vertebrae, sacrum and the coccyx give you the power. When you dance, skip and even walk, these parts help to keep you balanced.

In between each vertebra are small disks made of **cartilage**. These disks keep the vertebrae from rubbing against one another, and they also act as your spine's natural shock absorbers. When you jump in the air, the disks give your vertebrae the cushioning they need.

- There are more than 20 bones in each foot.

- The only jointless bone in our body is the hyoid bone in the throat.

- Babies are born with 300 bones, but by adulthood, the number is reduced to 206.

- The hardest bone in the human body is the jawbone. A bone is actually stronger than steel.

- We are about 1 cm taller in the morning than in the evening, due to the compression of the cartilage disks.

- Most people have lower back pain. This is because the lower back bears the weight of the upper body. It also twists and bends more than the upper back.

- If you get back pain after a small movement, such as picking up a book from the floor, you could have a slipped disc or a joint problem in your spine.

Chapter - 6

THE MUSCULAR SYSTEM

Each and every movement of the human body, from a wink to a heartbeat is produced by muscles. Muscles can be categorised as skeletal muscles, smooth muscles and cardiac muscles. All muscles are made up of fibres that contract to produce a pull.

Muscles at the front of the body are responsible for our facial expressions, movement of our heads, bending of the elbow, etc.

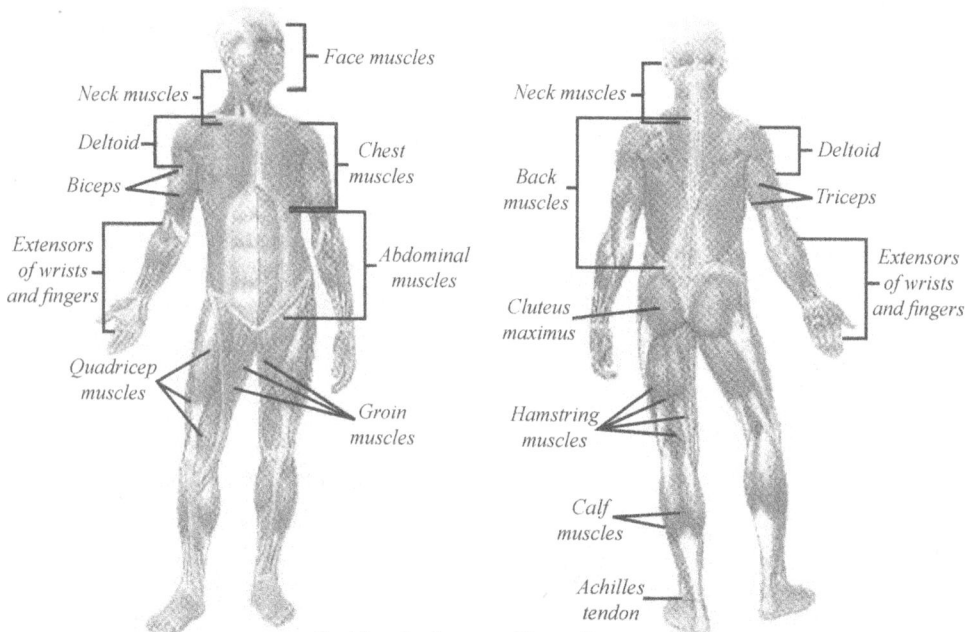

Face muscles
Neck muscles
Deltoid
Biceps
Chest muscles
Extensors of wrists and fingers
Abdominal muscles
Quadricep muscles
Groin muscles

Neck muscles
Back muscles
Deltoid
Triceps
Extensors of wrists and fingers
Cluteus maximus
Hamstring muscles
Calf muscles
Achilles tendon

The Muscular System in Human Beings

These muscles are called the **front muscles**. **Rear muscles** of the body, on the other hand, keep the head upright, steady the shoulders, bend knees, point toes downwards, etc.

The various kinds of muscles are:

Skeletal Muscles

These muscles are attached to the bones of the skeleton, which they pull to help us move around. Long and cylindrical fibres run parallel to each other. These can be up to 30 cm long. These fibres are bundled together to form muscles. These are attached to the bones by strong cords called the **tendons**. These muscles obey the instructions of the nervous system.

Smooth Muscles

These muscles are responsible for moving food around the intestines. These are tightly packed and layered sheets of muscle fibres and are found in hollow organs, such as the intestines, bladder, etc. in the intestine. They perform the job of pushing food around, whereas in the bladder, they help in the expulsion of the urine. These muscles contract slowly and their movements cannot be controlled voluntarily.

Cardiac Muscles

Cardiac muscles are extremely important as they perform the job of keeping the heart pumping. They are found solely in the walls of the heart. These muscle fibres form a branching

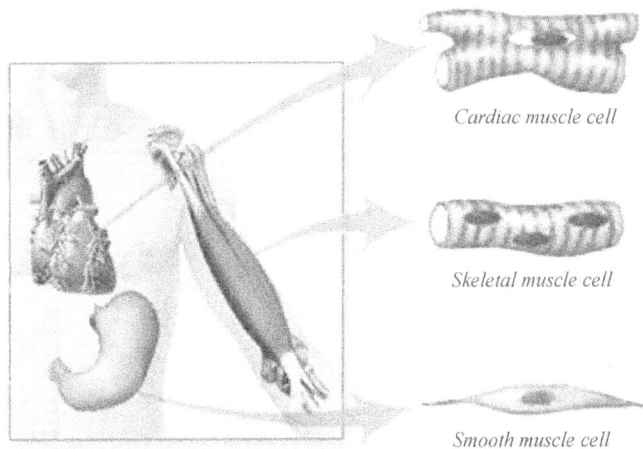

Cardiac muscle cell

Skeletal muscle cell

Smooth muscle cell

network that automatically contracts, without any stoppage. It is remarkable how these muscles never tire and constantly pump blood all around the body. However, the rate at which these muscles contract depends on the commands received by the nervous system which is a reflection of the body's demands.

Quick Facts

- The buttock muscle is the biggest muscle of the body.
- The tongue alone has around 16 separate muscles.
- There are three types of muscles found in the human body. They are: cardiac, smooth and skeletal.
- Cardiac muscles are called the heart muscles.
- The skeletal muscles form 40% of the body weight.
- The smooth muscles are in the digestive tract.
- One can barely live without muscles.

Chapter - 7

THE SKIN

The human skin is extremely vital to the body as it acts as a *protective overcoat* for the body. It is like a barrier between the vulnerable and delicate tissues of our body and the harsh and ever-changing conditions of the outside world. Some of the few roles played by our skin include *preventing water loss* and *invasion of germ cells*. Moreover, it also repairs itself constantly and enables us to *sense the surroundings* which we inhabit.

The skin is made up of a lot of layers. The uppermost layer of the human skin is majorly composed of dead cells. These dead cells are filled with a tough, water-proof substance called the **keratin**.

Cross-Section of the Human Skin

A section of the human skin, if analysed, reveals that it has two parts. These are the **epidermis** and the **dermis**.

While the epidermis is water resistant and germ–proof, protecting us against the harmful rays of the sun, the dermis is a

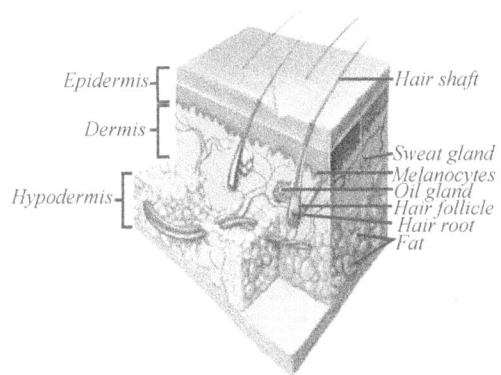

Cross-Section of the Human Skin

thicker layer, containing the *blood vessels*, *sensory receptors* and the *sweat glands*.

It is interesting to know that the flat, scaly cells in the upper epidermis are constantly removed and these are replaced by the cells at the base of the epidermis, which constantly multiply to serve the purpose.

Moreover, the epidermis contains cells that move upwards, dying, flattening and filling with **keratin**, while they do so. On the other hand, the dermis contains living cells and fibres that help the skin to stretch and recoil.

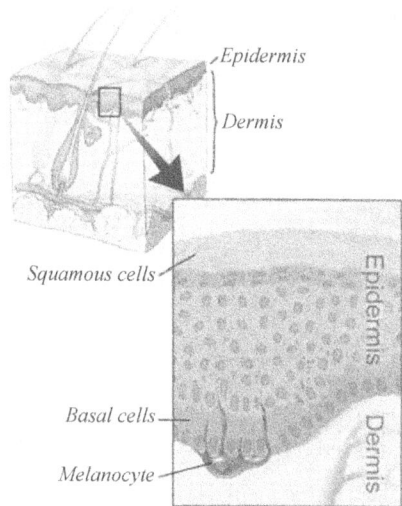

Epidermis and Dermis of Human Skin

Sweat

Sweat produced by our body is a salty liquid that comes from the sweat glands in the dermis. The main purpose of sweat is to maintain a stable body temperature. In hot temperatures, the dermis releases sweat to the surface of the skin, which then gets evaporated, providing coolness to the body, hence, maintaining a stable body temperature.

Skin Colour

There are special cells present in the epidermis that produce a brown pigment called **melanin**. This pigment filters out the harmful **ultraviolet** rays of the sun, in order

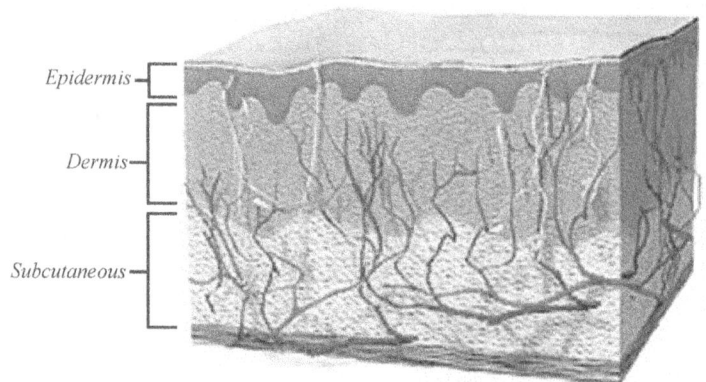

Layers of Human Skin

to protect the skin damage. It is melanin, along with the blood flowing through the dermis that provides the skin, its colour.

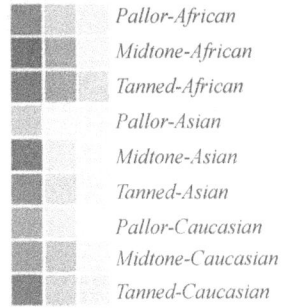

Pallor-African
Midtone-African
Tanned-African
Pallor-Asian
Midtone-Asian
Tanned-Asian
Pallor-Caucasian
Midtone-Caucasian
Tanned-Caucasian

Skin Colours

Quick Facts

- It is the largest organ in your body and protects your body from damage. An average adult's skin spans 21 square feet, weighs nine pounds, and contains more than 11 miles of blood vessels.

- The skin releases as much as three gallons of sweat a day in hot weather.

- Vitamin D is manufactured in the skin and is essential for digesting milk.

- The reason our lips are red is because the skin on the lips is very thin and the blood vessels show through.

- Every square inch of the human body has about 19,000,000 skin cells.

- Skin comes in different colours – The colour of someone's skin depends on the pigment that is in their skin; people with darker pigment have darker skin. People with darker skin don't tan as much as people with paler skin, because tanning is the formation of melanin.

Chapter - 8

THE HAIR

The entire human body is covered with hair. Some places that don't have hair include the *lips*, the *palms of the hands*, and the *soles of the feet*.

Some of the hair on the human body is easy to see, like the hair on the eyebrows, head, arms, and legs. But other hair, like that on your cheek, is almost invisible.

Depending on its location on the body, hair performs various functions. The hair on the head keeps it warm and provides cushioning to the skull. Similarly, eyelashes protect the eyes by decreasing the amount of light and dust that go into them and eyebrows protect the eyes from sweat dripping down from your forehead.

Where does the hair come from?

Whether hair is growing out of the head, arm, or ankle, it all rises out of the skin in the same way. It starts at the hair root, which is beneath the skin

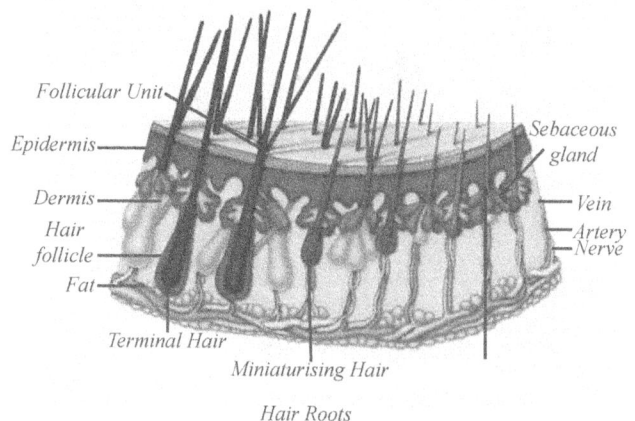

Follicular Unit

Epidermis

Dermis

Hair follicle

Fat

Terminal Hair

Miniaturising Hair

Hair Roots

Sebaceous gland

Vein

Artery

Nerve

where cells come together to form the **keratin**. The root is inside a **follicle**, a small tube in the skin.

As the hair begins to grow, it pushes up from the root and out of the follicle, through the skin where it can be seen. Blood vessels present at the base of every follicle feed the hair root to nurture it. However, it is astonishing that once the hair is at the skin's surface, the cells within the strand of hair aren't alive anymore. The hair you see on every part of your body contains **dead cells**.

Nearly every hair follicle is attached to a **sebaceous gland**, which is also known as the *oil gland*. These produce oil, which makes the hair shiny.

You have more than *100,000 hairs on your head*, but you lose some every day. About 50 to 100 hairs fall out each day, while you're washing your hair, brushing or combing it, or just sitting still.

Hair Colour

The hair colour comes from a pigment called **melanin**. It is the substance that gives hair and skin its pigment. The lighter someone's hair, the less melanin there is. A person with brown or black hair has much more melanin than someone with blond or red hair. Some hair follicles are structured in a way that produces *curly hair*, whereas others send out *straight hair*.

Follicles also determine if your hair will be *thick and coarse* or *thin and fine*.

Hair Care

With hair, the main thing is keeping it clean. Some people wash their hair every day, but others do it just once or twice a week. It depends on your hair and what kind of things you've been doing, like exercising or swimming.

- The female hair grows more slowly than the male hair.
- The lifespan of a human hair is 3 to 7 years on an average.
- Cutting hair does not influence its growth.
- Wet hair should not be rubbed since hair is very sensitive.
- Generally, a hair strand's lifespan is five and a half years.
- Hair grows faster in summer than in winter and more in day than at night.
- We lose around 50 to 100 strands of hair each day.

Chapter - 9

THE FINGERNAILS

Fingernails are ideal for gripping objects and scratching itches. They are clear protective plates and prevent damage to the sensitive part of our upper fingertips.

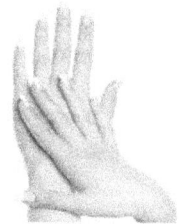

Fingure Nails

Fingernails are produced by living skin cells in the finger. They consist of several parts, which include the *nail plate*, which is the visible part of the nail, the *nail bed*, which is the skin beneath the nail plate, the *cuticle*, which is the tissue that overlaps the plate and rims the base of the nail, the *nail folds*, which is the skin folds that frame and support the nail on three sides, the *lunula*, which is the whitish half-moon at the base of the nail and the *matrix*, which is the hidden part of the nail unit under the *cuticle*.

Fingernails grow from the matrix. The nails are composed largely of *keratin*, which is a hardened protein and is also found in our skin and hair. As new cells grow in

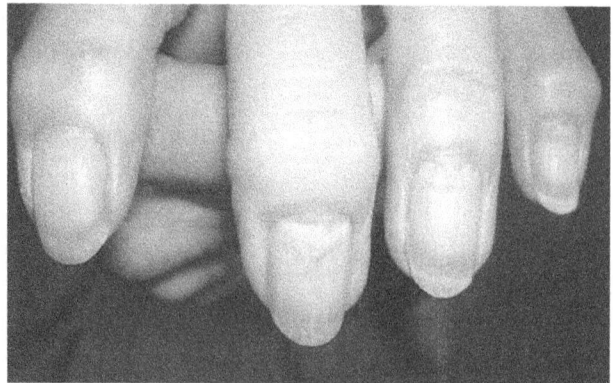

Fingernails grow from the matrix

the matrix, the older cells are removed, compacted and take on the familiar flattened, hardened form of the fingernail. The cells that make nails die, flatten and fill with keratin as they are pushed forward from the nail's root.

It is interesting to know that the average growth rate for nails is 0.1 mm each day (or 1 centimetre in 100 days). However, the exact rate of nail growth depends on numerous factors, which include the age and sex of the individual and also the time of year. Fingernails generally grow faster in young people, in males, and in the summer.

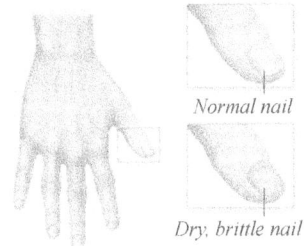

Normal nail

Dry, brittle nail

It is another interesting fact that fingernails grow faster than toenails. The fingernails on the right hand of a right handed person grow faster than those on their left hand, and vice versa.

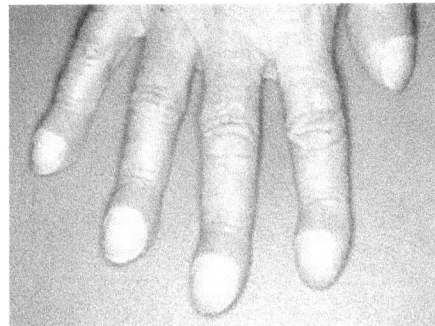

Brittle Nails

Our fingernails tell a lot about our body's health. Many of the body's deficiencies, etc. are reflected in our nails. For example, **brittle nails** reflect a *deficiency of calcium*, whereas **yellow nails** depict serious *liver problems*. **Blue nails** are a sign of **circulatory problem**.

Hence, it is extremely important to keep a regular check on our overall health as it is evident that the entire body suffers due to problems that are concentrated in only one part.

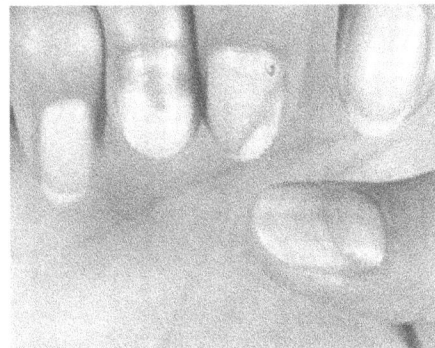

Yellow Nails

Quick Facts

- About 1cm of nail takes 100 days to grow.

- Men's nails grow faster than a woman's nails.

- Nails are actually the same as hair. Both hair and nails are made of the same protein, called keratin.

- The nail plates are dead cells and contrary to the popular belief, they don't breathe. So they don't require oxygen. However, the nail beds and the cuticles are live cells and they do need oxygen, vitamins and minerals.

- Nails don't sweat. The nail bed does not have sweat glands, so it can't perspire. It is the skin around the nails that gets sweaty.

- Nails grow at the rate of 0.1 mm daily (or 1 cm in every 100 days). So, for a finger nail to grow again completely, it takes between 4 and 6 months. For toe nails, the period of complete growth is 12 to 18 months.

- Men's nails grow faster than women's nails.

- Finger nails for both genders grow faster than toe nails.

- Toe nails are about twice thicker than finger nails.

- The fastest growing nail is on the middle finger. The slowest – on the thumbnail.

- Seasons and weather also affect nail growth. Nails grow faster in warm climates and during daytime, than in cold climates and at night.

Exercises

I. Answer the following questions.

1. How many organ systems are there in the human body?

2. What are the basic constituents of the human body?

3. What is a cell and what are the different kinds of cells present in a human body?

4. Describe briefly the following types of cells with diagrams:

   (i) Red Blood Cells(RBCs) (ii) White Blood Cells(WBCs)

   (iii) Nerve Cells

5. Where are the Epithelial Cells present and what are their functions?

6. Why is the human blood red in colour? What are the chief constituents of the blood?

7. Draw a diagram of the brain and label its different parts. Also, explain each part of the brain briefly with its functions.

8. How many sense organs do we have? Draw a diagram of each of them and explain them briefly.

9. Explain the Respiratory System in human beings with the help of a diagram.

10. Explain all about the Digestive System in human beings with the help of a diagram.

II. Fill in the blanks with suitable words.

1. The _____ filter and take the waste out of the blood, and make urine.

2. The length of the small intestine is about _____ feet long.

3. Our _____ can hold up to 1.5 litres of water or liquid material.

4. _____ to and from the brain travel as fast as 170 miles per hour.

5. The size of the _____ is about the same size of a fist.

6. The heart is a very special kind of _____. Its job is to send blood all over the body.

7. The human heart is divided into four chambers. The upper two chambers are called as _____ and the lower chambers are called _____.

8. A bundle of muscles extends from the floor of the mouth to form the _____.

9. Nutrition can be broadly categorised into three types of food, such as: _____, _____ and _____.

10. _____ and _____ are part of the natural immunity system where the body is trying to eject pathogens and irritants from the respiratory system.

III. Match the two columns correctly.

A	B
1. If your saliva cannot dissolve something,	is present in our ears.
2. The smallest bone in the human body, called the stirrup	you cannot taste it.

3. We lose half a litre of water a day   206 bones.
4. The human body consists of   through breathing.

IV. Multiple Choice Questions (MCQs)

1. Hair is the fastest growing tissue in the body, second only to the

   a. Bone marrow.   b. Blood.   c. Fingernails.

2. The fastest growing nail is on the middle finger. The slowest is the

   a. Ring finger.   b. Little finger.

   c. Thumb nail.

3. Vitamin D is manufactured in the skin and is essential for

   a. digesting curd.   b. digesting vegetables.

   c. digesting milk.

4. The buttock muscle is the _____ muscle of the body.

   a. smallest   b. biggest   c. medium

5. The skeletal muscles form _____ of the body weight.

   a. 40 percent   b. 50 percent

   c. 60 percent

6. The first seven vertebrae at the top are called the

   a. thoracic vertebrae.   b. cervical vertebrae.

   c. abdominal vertebrae.

7. Humans have over _____ moveable and semi-moveable joints in their bodies.

   a. 250   b. 240

   c. 230   d. 260

8. After eating too much, your hearing becomes_____ sharp.

    a. more   b. less

    c. the same   d. none of these

9. The backbone or the vertebral column, consists of a long chain of _____bones, each individually known as a vertebra.

    a. 40   b. 33

    c. 48   d. 36

10. We breathe around _____of air each minute.

    a. 4.5 litres   b. 5.5 litres

    c. 6.5 litres   d. 8.5 litres

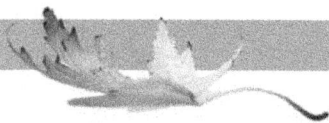

Glossary

Palate: The roof of the mouth

Pharynx: Throat

Uvula: Dangling flesh at the back of the mouth, contained in the soft palate

Tonsils: Clumps of tissue on both sides of the throat that help fight infections

Papillae: Tiny bumps on the tongue that contain the taste buds

Amylase: Digestive enzyme that starts the breakdown of carbohydrates even before food enters the stomach

Orbicularis oris: Major lip muscle that allows lips' mobility

Pulp: The innermost portion of teeth

Dentin: Hard, yellow substance which surround the pulp

Enamel: This forms the outermost layer of the crown, and protects the teeth

Cementum: A bony layer which covers the outside of the root and keeps the tooth in place

Cartilage: Soft and flexible material which is found in babies' bones

Bone Marrow: Soft, spongy material found at the centre of the bones; new blood cells are created here

Periosteum: Outer surface of the bones; contains nerve and blood cells

Compact bone: A layer next to the periosteum

Cancellous bone: A spongy layer within the compact bone

Sclera: The white part of the eyeball

Cornea: A transparent part which sits in front of the coloured part of the eye

Iris: The coloured part of the eye

Pupil: An opening through which light enters the eye

Anterior chamber: A space that is filled with a special fluid that keeps the eye healthy

Lens: That part of the eye that focuses light rays to the retina

Retina: This changes the light rays into nerve signals and sends them to the brain

Vitreous: It is situated behind the retina and is the biggest part of the eye

Vitreous Humour: Clear, jelly-like material in the vitreous; light shines through this to the back of the eye

Rods and cones: These are used by the retina to process light

Lacrimal glands: These glands produce tears

Pinna or Auricle: The outer ear

Ossicles: Three, tiny bones in the ear which help the sound in moving towards the inner ear

Cochlea: Small tube in the inner ear where sound waves are converted into nerve signals for the brain

Vertebral Column: Spine or backbone

Vertebrae/ Vertebra: A chain of ring-shaped bones in the spine

Cervical Vertebrae: The first seven vertebrae which support the head and neck

Thoracic Vertebrae: These hold the ribs of the chest primarily in place

Lumbar Vertebrae: The five vertebrae below the thoracic vertebrae

Sacrum: It is made of five vertebrae which are fused to form one single bone; situated below the lumbar

Coccyx: One bone made of the four fused vertebrae, below the sacrum

Cardiovascular System: The circulatory system which regulates the blood flow all over the body

Atria: The top or upper two chambers of the heart which carry blood to the heart from the different parts of the body and the lungs

Ventricles: The bottom or the lower two chambers of the heart. They carry blood from the heart to all the various parts of the body including the lungs

Septum: The thick wall of muscle which separates the left and right side of the heart

Mitral valve and Tricuspid valve: This allows the blood flow from the atria to the ventricles

Aortic valve and Pulmonary valve: They control the flow of the blood as it leaves the heart

Arteries: Blood vessels that carry blood away from the heart

Veins: They carry blood back to the heart

Pulse: Rhythmic expansion of arteries

Synovial fluid: This is a special fluid that helps the joints move freely

Ligaments: These make the bones hold on to the joints

Meninges: The layers of membranes which cushion the vertebrae

Central Nervous System (CNS): It receives information from

the brain and sends information to the Peripheral Nervous System (PNS)

Peripheral Nervous System (PNS): Various nerves branching out from the spinal cord to the entire body

Cerebrospinal fluid: This helps to protect the nerve tissues, keep it healthy, and remove the waste products

Neurons: Tiny cells which relay information to each other to perform various functions

Sensory Neurons: They send information from the sensory receptors towards the Central Nervous System

Motor Neurons: They send information from the Central Nervous System to the muscles or glands

Sensory Nervous System: This sends information to the Central Nervous System (CNS) from our internal body organs or from the external stimuli

Motor Nervous System: It carries information from the CNS to the different organs, muscles and glands

Somatic Nervous System: It controls the skeletal muscles as well as the external sensory organs, such as the eyes, nose, ears, etc.

Autonomic Nervous System: This controls the involuntary muscles, such as the smooth and the cardiac muscles

Sympathetic Nervous System: It controls activities that require high amounts of energy. It prepares the body for any kind of sudden stress or tension

Parasympathetic Nervous System: This controls activities that conserve the body's energy and help it to rest

Excretory System: This removes waste products from the body

Kidneys: They filter and take the waste out of the blood and make urine. These are the main organs of the excretory system

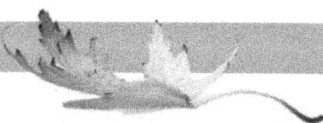

Ureters: These are tubes that carry the urine to the bladder

Bladder: A bag that collects the urine

Urethra: A tube that carries the urine out of the body

Renal: Anything in the body related to the kidneys

Nephrons: Tiny filters which remove waste products

Homeostasis: It is the balance of the volume of fluids and minerals in the body done by the kidneys

Dialysis: People with malfunctioning kidneys often have to go through this process, where they are hooked up to a machine that filters their blood and acts as an artificial kidney

SELF IMPROVEMENT
(आत्म विकास)

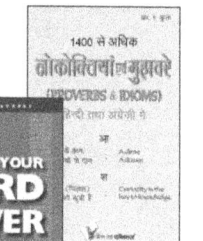

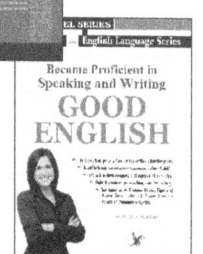

ENGLISH IMPROVEMENT
(अंग्रेजी सुधार)

Modern Letter Writing Course

SUCCESS 2020

The Success Failure

क्या आप माँ बनने जा रही है...?
मातृकला

ENGLISH GRAMMAR AND USAGE

ENGLISH VOCABULARY Made Easy

मॉडर्न लेटर राइटिंग कोर्स

How To Become a Successful Speaker & Presenter

सफल वक्ता एवं वाक्-प्रवीण कैसे बनें

HUMOR US MIDDLES

IMPROVE YOUR VOCABULARY

SPOKEN ENGLISH

पर्सनैलिटी डेवलपमेंट कोर्स

75 Ways to Happiness

Changing Perspective Changing Life

AUTISM

PICTURE DICTIONARY Aa

1400 से अधिक लोकोक्तियाँ व मुहावरे (PROVERBS & IDIOMS)

IMPROVE YOUR WORD POWER

MEMORY DEVELOPMENT COURSE

बॉडी लैंग्वेज

क्या आप जानते हैं

सफलता के 51 मंत्र

BUSINESS ENGLISH

Become Proficient in Speaking and Writing GOOD ENGLISH

STRESS MANAGEMENT (तनाव मुक्ति)

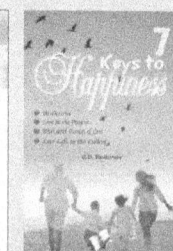

STRESS ZONE

PEACE of MIND In Unique Verses

मानसिक शांति के रहस्य

KEY to STRESS FREE LIVING

Know Thyself

The Art of Happy Living

7 Keys to Happiness

CAREER & BUSINESS MANAGEMENT
(कॅरियर एण्ड बिजनेस मैनेजमेंट)

JOB RELATED
(नौकरी सम्बन्धी)

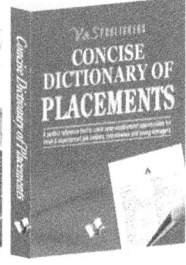

STUDENT DEVELOPMENT/LEARNING
(छात्र विकास/लर्निंग)

JOKES
(हास्य)

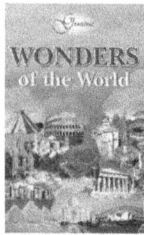

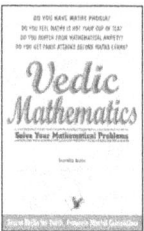

MAGIC & FACT (जादू एवं तथ्य)

MUSIC (संगीत)

COMPUTER

Quiz Books
(प्रश्नोत्तरी की पुस्तकें)

MYSTERIES
(रहस्य)

DRAWING BOOKS (ड्राइंग बुक्स)

BIOGRAPHIES (आत्म कथाएँ)

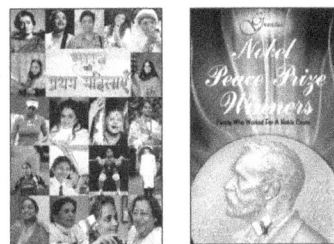

QUOTES/SAYINGS (अनमोल/सूक्तिवाणी)

PUZZLES (पहेलियां)

ACTIVITIES BOOK (एक्टिविटीज बुक)

Contact us at sales@vspublishers.com

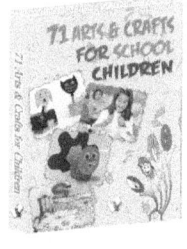

POPULAR SCIENCE
(लोकप्रिय विज्ञान)

FICTION
(उपन्यास, कथा साहित्य)

Save ₹ 50/-
Pay ₹ 850/- instead of
₹ 850/- for complete
set of 17 book price
₹ 50/- each

FREE CD

Set Code:
02122S

101 + 10 नए
साइंस गेम्स

101 + 10 New
SCIENCE
GAMES

चिल्ड्रेन्स साइंस एन्साइक्लोपीडिया

Children's
SCIENCE
ENCYCLOPEDIA

Fully Colour

CLASSIC SERIES GRADED READERS (क्लासिक श्रृंखला)

New

Graded Reader

Gift Pack

Save ₹ 300/-
Pay ₹ 1200/- instead of
₹ 1500/- for complete
Set of 10 books price
₹ 150/- each

SCIENCE FICTION STORIES

SHERLOCK HOLMES STORIES

TERROR STORIES

SUPERNATURAL STORIES

HUMOR STORIES

LOVE STORIES

DETECTIVE STORIES

GHOST STORIES

SHERLOCK HOLMES STORIES

SHERLOCK HOLMES STORIES

CHILDREN TALES
(बच्चों की कहानियाँ)

Interesting Tales for Children

बच्चों के लिए रोचक कहानियाँ

Legendary Tales for Children

पौराणिक कहानियाँ

Jungle Tales for Children

जंगल की कहानियाँ

Folk Tales for Children

बच्चों के लिए अनमोल कहानियाँ

Ramayana Tales for Children

बच्चों के लिए रामायण की कहानियाँ

TALES & STORIES
(कथा एवं कहानियाँ)

PANCHATANTRA

PANCHATANTRA

PANCHATANTRA

PANCHATANTRA

All Books Fully Coloured

पंचतंत्र

पंचतंत्र

पंचतंत्र

पंचतंत्र

Moral Stories NEW

Wisdom Tales

शिक्षाप्रद कहानियाँ

कहावतों की कहानियां

कहावत

पंचतंत्र की कथाएं

Interesting Stories to Learn PROVERBS

HINDI LITERATURE
(हिन्दी साहित्य)

प्रेमचन्द प्रसिद्ध कहानियाँ

श्रेष्ठ साहित्यकारों की प्रसिद्ध कहानियाँ

www.ingramcontent.com/pod-product-compliance
Lightning Source LLC
Chambersburg PA
CBHW081419270326
41931CB00015B/3336